5

Don & Martha
Don thank you for
all your counseling and
help over the years.

Martha,
Thank you for the
grace and hospitality
you have always shown.

May God keep you
healthy and well.

Sincerely,
Darcie
Cooper

The
Reality
of
Bipolar
Disorder

My Story of Faith, Strength, and Hope

Darcie Cooper

authorHOUSE®

AuthorHouse™
1663 Liberty Drive
Bloomington, IN 47403
www.authorhouse.com
Phone: 1 (800) 839-8640

Published by AuthorHouse 10/07/2015

ISBN: 978-1-5049-5164-7 (sc)
ISBN: 978-1-5049-5005-3 (hc)
ISBN: 978-1-5049-5163-0 (e)

Library of Congress Control Number: 2015915767

Print information available on the last page.

Author's Note

Dear reader:

Thank you for the opportunity to present my story to you. My story is meant to be an easy read for people in need of help and support. Tragedy was a part of my life for many years; it tested my bipolar illness to the brink of madness and insanity. Bipolar disorder is a horrible, devastating disease that takes thousands of lives every year due to suicide. It is the number-four disability in America. Even though there has been a lot of tragedy in my life while I've suffered with bipolar disorder, my story of triumph is about how I have been able to stay alive—and stay sane—through extreme circumstances. With my story of survival through all my adversities and challenges, I hope to give you, the reader of my book—and your families—the same faith and hope that have brought me to where I am today. Yes, bipolar is a grave up-and-down disease, but as I explain in my personal story, there are effective ways to cope with this illness. I hope my story will compel you to find your way, too.

To the families of those who are diagnosed with bipolar disorder (also called manic-depression):

You suffer immensely at the sight of your beautiful loved ones, wishing they could have faith, strength, and peace. You, too, can be a part of their faith and peace, and keep it alive. Grab onto it, claim it, and keep it close to your heart. This disease is a journey, and the twists and turns are tumultuous; but don't let it cause you to doubt your faith and hope. Just by being by their side and loving them, you will immensely improve their chances of having a more stable life.

—Darcie Cooper, Summer 2015

Preface

My story is one of tragedy, loss, poor physical health, and bipolar disorder. I believe I have been led by God's Spirit to present my story to others who are suffering from this madness of bipolar, and to assure you that we can have hope—through all of life's circumstances. God wants us to know that we do not have to resort to self-harm or suicide.

Even though we may have bipolar, and go through the extreme challenges it poses upon us each and every day, if we are rigorous about our medications and keeping an appropriate lifestyle, we can effectively stabilize the disease and choose a good life. God does not want us to suffer. He has made medications to help us through, and He is with us.

Strange but true, we are being made stronger through pain. I will not pity myself. At times, under great duress, I cry out to God, *Why? Why this disease*? I know He has his reasons and I have to respect them.

My book is simply my life story—my own journey including its many obstacles. Each person's experience with this disease will be different. My objective, my entire life since the diagnosis—as it surely is with anyone who is given the diagnosis of bipolar—has been to stay sane. Since our destinies are different, and they call us at different times of our lives, we must flow with what has been given. My story may have more or less heartbreak and heartache than any other; but the madness of the disease is always there. All our stories and journeys are ours. Each of our journeys is easier or harder than another's, but they are ours alone. Take hold of your own personal journey. Make peace with it. Peace is truth.

With Great Thanks

To my true loves, Jacqueline and Brooke. You have seen more than your fair share of chaos, madness, and sadness. You have witnessed how devastating this disorder can be. Thank you for being my angels, and always loving me unconditionally.

—Mom

Dedication

To my grandmother:
Your sweet spirit and
love gave me the courage
to believe I could
accomplish anything.

ဆ

To my dear
psychologists, therapists, and social workers
who have encouraged and inspired me
to tell my story: I thank you for
having faith in me.

ဆ

To my loved ones,
you who have passed on before me:
I miss you and love you with all my
heart and soul. I long to see
you, but not today.
Today is God's day.
He has a plan for me.
I accept, and He will call me
to be with you in His time.
My never-ending love.

Words of Encouragement

Being broken is the first step to being healed.

I have heard your prayers, and seen your tears; I will heal you.—2 Kings 20:5

Accept yourself as you are. Expose yourself to light, and darkness will fade.

Embrace today with a fearless heart.

When we want our suffering to end, we let the Spirit in.

I can live with the past just as it was. I can live with the future as it may be.

The meaning of life is the meaning you give it.

It is okay to accept the outcome of today, whatever form it may take.

I can accept change, even when accompanied by pain.

Let us breathe and trust. It is with courage we become free.

When the weight feels like too much, and it seems like there's no one we can trust, let the Spirit set you free.

Stay full of hope and full of dreams: Keep them alive.

A Word about the Graphics

I have placed this symbol ✳ at the top of each page of my narrative, because it is very dear to me. This symbol is the Morning Star: a symbol of hope and guidance. It has been shared with us by Native Americans. Dealing with bipolar, I know I can use that ancient wisdom, and think upon this star with each new day.

Table of Contents

Chapter One

Family of Origin: Destiny

This chapter explores how the stage is set for what our future holds. You may or may not relate; but I know now that, without a doubt, this is where my predestined journey was established, playing out as my reality later in life.

Our family of origin plays a large part in whether or not we will be diagnosed bipolar, schizophrenic, or with some other mental illness. Genetics play the biggest role in our illness. In my case, mental illness started on my grandmother's side of the family. My grandmother's first husband was thought to have been bipolar; he had a very obvious mental illness. He was an extreme alcoholic and was abusive to my grandmother. My grandmother divorced him when my mother was twelve years old. Sometime after the divorce, my grandfather committed suicide by driving his car off of a cliff.

My mother suffered from some minor depression. I believe it was due partly to never really knowing her father or any of his family. He was not around much for her to ever get to know him.

My mother's brother was diagnosed with schizophrenia when he was eighteen years of age. My grandmother did not know what to do with him. He was extremely unmanageable. She had no choice but to commit him to The Mental Institution in Oregon, where he remained for over 30 years, and where he was horribly mistreated.

After my uncle was at the institution 31 years, the FDA discovered a drug called Clozaril. After he had been on a regimen of Clozaril for one year, he was finally doing very well. He was released back to his home town, where he was placed in an adult foster home. He seemed to do well there. He loved to walk around town, and he had his favorite places to go. Often times I would see him in town at a little market, which was one of his daily stopping and resting places. He would be standing, sitting, or leaning on the side of the building. I would stop and give him five dollars. I was never able to make any sense of what my uncle was saying. I pretended to understand, for his sake. Drugs over the years had affected his speech tremendously, and he drooled a lot.

One day when I saw him at the market, the manager came out and asked me, "Ma'am, is he bothering you?" I answered no rather sharply, and explained that he was my uncle. The man was very surprised and went back inside. That was one of the first steps along my journey. I accept my uncle for who he was, not a transient, as others saw him. He was a very sweet man who deserved respect, like us all.

In foster care, my uncle was given an allowance every day for coffee and cigarettes. He led a very simple life until his death at the age of 60. He passed from pneumonia and emphysema. My grandmother was devastated. She felt guilty, wishing she'd had more time with him. She wanted to make up for the three decades that she was not present in his life; but the fact is, there was not anything she could have done for him in those years, nor anything much after he came back home.

Whether or not mental illness started one hundred years ago or forty years ago in our family, it will shape and determine our lives. My mother's family's genes were passed down to her. She never had any symptoms of mental illness. However, she was often unavailable to my three brothers and me when we were growing up. Our lives were never normal. There was constant chaos in our home. At the age of 19, my youngest brother was diagnosed with schizophrenia. Later in life, I was diagnosed with Bipolar 1 Disorder with Psychosis.

I am quite capable of living on my own. However, my brother is living in a foster home. He will not take medications, and is frequently hospitalized for bizarre behaviors—such as running down the highway, without clothing, shouting that he was being deported. At that point, the police took him to the hospital, where they put him in the Psychiatric Ward. He has been hospitalized like this several times. In Oregon, if patients refuse medication but do not pose a threat to themselves, the institution lets them go.

My brother lives a truly horrible existence. He believes that Satan is always speaking to him. He is very violent toward televisions and windows, he believes people are watching him through the windows, and that the television and Satan are speaking to him and telling him to kill people. He has never hurt anyone, except in elementary school, where he did get into a lot of fights and got expelled.

No matter what you do or try, nothing will work without medication.

The diagnosis of Bipolar 1 Disorder with Psychosis is described as having severe episodes with hallucinations and delusions. During a psychotic episode, I will not reason with anyone, and will at times end up in the hospital. This is very rare. But if it happens, I have learned a lot of ways to cope during these horrible times. Psychosis causes false fixed beliefs, meaning I can take what someone says and instantly my mind goes to thinking that person is out to get me. Hallucinations and delusions are always present with episodes of psychosis. Some are extreme and terrifying, while others are more mild. They are normally due to a change in my Lithium level. A change can happen if I have a difference in my routine, or experience stress or a lack of sleep. Alcohol can be a big factor as well, so I try to stay away from it completely. Under the care of my doctor, who adjusts my Lithium, I will level out most times within two to three days. Once it is corrected, I return to a sane state of mind, and all is normal again. Thankfully these episodes are few and far between.

Every manic episode will also cause psychotic symptoms. I have learned to live with them. They are difficult when they happen, because they seem all too real. I keep telling myself during the episode: *This too shall pass. I have been here before and it will level out again.* Even though I am aware, and tell myself that it will be okay, I am still terrified that there may come a time when I won't ever level out again.

I have two daughters, and I also try to help others—mostly elderly people, with tasks such as grocery shopping, light housekeeping, and companionship. Elderly people can become very demanding of my time, so I have to set boundaries with them. They don't take that very well. When they don't, I have to let them go. People have to respect my time, as I respect theirs. Having a very severe illness can make these seemingly simple things all but impossible to do at times.

When I speak of stability, I am speaking of periods of time when I am *not* actively suicidal, manic, or depressed. I will always suffer from irritability, aggression, and agitation; this is the disease. I do not want to even try to fathom what my life would be like without Lithium. Most likely, I would not be on this Earth. Later in life, I am hopeful that I will see my symptoms become less severe, as my stress level lowers when my children are both off to college and life is less demanding. A very loving relationship will also diminish episodes. I am very much an outdoors person, and I have someone in my life now who has the same interests. *Being in nature is God's natural medicine, and I will take it in to the fullest.*

I have listed in the back of this book some coping skills that are very helpful. I use them regularly, and they help me to get through most of the stress in my life. If I am stress-free, I am episode-free.

Bipolar illness is very complex. Any person who is Bipolar 1, Bipolar 2, or Bipolar 3 experiences varying degrees of racing thoughts and delusions. With my Bipolar 1 and Psychosis, it is hard for me to distinguish between mania and depression. Either one takes me to a state of insanity. When I am depressed, I still have extreme anger, irritability, and psychosis—which mimics mania in a lot of ways. Whatever type of bipolar a person suffers from, the symptoms are often debilitating, and can quickly become overwhelming. The symptoms of this grave disease vary widely from individual to individual, so medications must be customized for each person. Some individuals may just desire to sleep when they are depressed. When manic, they may still have some degree of control over their lives.

Chapter Two

Early Childhood: Chaos—Dark and Afraid

When do the earliest childhood memories start affecting an individual with bipolar disorder? I believe that bipolar can act in one of two ways. Of course the gene is there; however, professionals cannot predict when it may rear its ugly head. Some say that with a loving and stable home environment in the early years, bipolar will develop later in life. In a home filled with chaos, drama, and physical abuse, it may be more likely to manifest itself at a younger age, and possess different qualities, as in my case. This is my hypothesis, of course. I believe this disease is truly a mystery when it comes to predicting the level of bipolar symptoms an individual may suffer.

As a child I was paranoid all the time. I believe this was due to the way I was treated on a daily basis. I was also an extreme introvert. This was due to the chaos and drama that was a daily occurrence in my home. I have memories of my life beginning at six years of age. My brother Evan, the youngest, and I were closest in age and size. My grandmother and my mother dressed me like a boy. So, my youngest brother and I were dressed exactly the same. At the time, I thought it was normal. In the neighborhood I grew up in, there were not any girls to play with, just several boys. We lived on a very remote street out in the country, in a very small town. So as a girl I was treated exactly the same as a boy by all the neighbor kids. They would set me up to fight other boys, I would most always win. I was used to fighting with my brothers; it was a way of life for me. I did not like it, but I felt that I had to go along in order to have any interaction with the other kids. They were just using me to humiliate the other boy when I would win. This brought on a lot of embarrassment; I was always embarrassed to be a girl. I remember several nights praying to God to change me into a boy. I thought being a boy would protect me.

I was an easily influenced child. When I was eight years old, a neighbor started molesting me. Even at this young age, I knew something wasn't right but I felt powerless over him. He would threaten me that bad things would happen to me if I should tell anyone. This really scared me into keeping this dark secret. I felt unclean and afraid. He sodomized me in front of others. I did not know how to escape. My mother was so unavailable, I certainly would not tell her. This went on for many years. He did all kinds of horrible things to me, including raping me. Later in life, I am still disgusted. *How does a man rape a girl at such a young age?* I already felt awkward, and all these experiences just underlined my hatred towards life. The last time he touched me inappropriately was when I was 16, and only for a brief second. It happened in front of a girl I knew from school, which made me feel worse than I already did.

My father was an extreme alcoholic. On his way home from work, my father would stop at a little market a mile from our home, and buy a twelve-pack of beer. He would open one immediately and drive home. From there, he would go into his shop and drink until my mother called him in for dinner.

Dinner was full of torment. My mother could be very vicious. She would continuously tell my father how horrible we had behaved all day. He would fly into a rage, tear off his belt, and chase us one by one down the hallway to our bedrooms and whip us. My oldest brother remembers wetting his pants out of fear. It is very hard to explain how

I felt at this time. I was definitely humiliated, and I would cry and cry, and ask time and time again in my mind, *Why would they do this to us?* It did not make any sense. At times, often at the dinner table, my mother would reach over and slap me across the face. I assumed I had said something she disliked. I would become enraged, but I knew I could not show it, or she would slap me again. My rage grew towards my father as well. I realized something else after a while: My mother never slapped my brothers like that. I was very confused. I always felt that she hated me. My entire childhood was filled with fear, rage, disgust, and humiliation. Later in my teenage and adult life, my rage started to come out.

My home was always immersed in a circle of violence, guilt, and shame. Living this life made me start to dislike everyone. After school, I started climbing to the tops of trees so I could hide; or, I would climb to the top of a mountain where I could see our entire small valley, and have some peace. In this way, I was able to avoid my mother and brothers, so that I could stay out of trouble. I would wait at the top of the tree or mountain, until Mother would call Father in for dinner. I figured, that way, I was safe. She never paid much attention to where I was all day.

One day I purposely rode off on my motorcycle. I went up into the mountains. It was early in the day, when we had a day off of school. I did it just to see if she would ever come looking for me. She never did. Around dinner time I went home. She never even asked me one question about where I was.

It was a lonely life. I realized later in life that I was using the tree and the mountain as a way to escape as much fear, rejection, humiliation, and abuse as possible. My two brothers and I also started skipping school frequently. We would wait on the top of the mountain, where we could look down on our home to watch our mother leave for work. She had work doing some house-cleaning jobs. When she was away at work, we had relief from her wrath; but she was only working two days a week. For school the next day, I would write notes for my brothers and me, since I could write just like my mother. In those days, the schools never called home to see why you were absent. My brothers skipped a lot more often than I did. That is probably why I graduated high school, but they did not. Skipping school also helped me at times to avoid the abusive neighbor.

My mother continued to treat me like a boy, so I copied the boys. When I was 12 years old, I would run around with my shirt off like the boys in our neighborhood. Then a boy from school came along. I liked him, and asked him over after school. He was also 12. It was hot, so I had taken my shirt off. He left, and did not come over again. My aunt and cousins stepped in that day, and my aunt explained to me how inappropriate it was for a girl to act that way. She had three daughters. I was mortified and humiliated, and of course my rage was boiling up again. I did not know why my mother never even cared. My mother's behavior continued this way towards me for years. I knew I would never be able to please her, and I never did.

ɑ

As I became older, I was a recluse. I stayed away from everyone in junior high and high school. I did not have any friends, and at the time I did not want any. I was just a fly on the wall at school; I was there to graduate and start my life. I know some people who graduate and then they are afraid to live on their own. For me, it was different. I knew leaving home was my way out of misery.

All the way through school, from elementary to high school, the chaos still existed at home. My mother had attended several different churches over the years. She started attending a new church, and after she'd been attending for quite a while, she started making us go with her. The trip to church was 26 miles there and 26 miles home. My oldest brother was not required to come. He was six years older than I was, so she assumed he could make up his own mind. My mother's sister-in-law would always ride over with us. The trip was terrible. My brothers and I would fight like cats and dogs. My mother would threaten us with punishment on the way back. It happened every time. My mother would stop halfway home near a spot by the freeway under a big willow tree. She would make us all pick a branch, and she would start whipping us. It was humiliating in front of my aunt and passersby. I was now 13 years of age.

When we arrived home one day, and my Father was away at his brother's home, I could no longer contain my rage. I tackled my mother to the ground. My brothers had to pull me off of her. She would often allow my brothers to hold me down and spit in my face. She never cared when I would call her for help to make them get off of me; she would let them do it anyway. I was not going to spit in her face. I was far beyond that. I did know something about right and wrong.

I noticed about a week or so later that I had been suffering from depression for a period of about six weeks. I did not fully realize what it was doing to me; it brought out all kinds of emotions. I felt remorseful for a short period of time. After all, she was still my mother. Later in life, in therapy, I found out that it was then that I had experienced my first bipolar depression. It finally made sense—why this rage had to let itself out, and why the incident with my mother had happened. My therapist would assure me that a person can only take so much abuse, and this is all the more true if that person has bipolar. During this depression, I gained 15 pounds, not knowing why. Again, my mother never asked if anything were wrong. I made it through, and all of the weight in due course dropped off; but I had no idea this was a symptom of bipolar. Life for me at this point was full of rejection, disappointment, and other emotions I did not understand.

CR

Eventually, my luck started to turn. A new family started attending our church. The family consisted of the mother, father, and four daughters. I was delighted that they started inviting me for sleep-overs after church every weekend. (We went to church on Saturdays.) They would also invite me over during the week if school was out. Then, during the summer, sometimes I stayed for weeks at a time. When I would call home to ask if I could stay an extra week, my mother did not hesitate to say yes. Most of the time, the girls' mother would listen just to make sure it was okay. She was always surprised when my mother did not hesitate. She started becoming aware that my father was an alcoholic, and home was no place for me anyway. They made the best possible home for me. Their house was so inviting. It radiated love—no chaos or drama. The father and mother were kind and gentle to me. I finally felt that someone cared about me, for the first time in my life.

The church started a youth group, and I started getting very involved along with the other girls. Our church was a large denomination. I believe it was called The Worldwide Church of God founded by Herbert W. Armstrong, with churches all over the United States. Basketball and volleyball teams were started. The four girls and I all became involved. We started playing in tournaments all over Oregon, and a couple in Washington, too. This was a very exciting time for me. It turns out, I was a pretty good player as well. I played basketball and volleyball until I was 18. At the end of the basketball season, when I was 18, the basketball coach suggested to me that I should move on and play for the College of The Siskiyous. Unfortunately, that would never happen, with my self-esteem still so low, even though I knew I was a very good player—and with my parents being who they were. They did not care about college, let alone basketball. I hid my sadness. I knew it would have been a dream come true. And I knew I would never get an opportunity like that again.

During the time period of church and school, I started working at a pizza parlor. I needed to buy my own car to get back and forth to where the youth group and this other family were. I had to stay away from my family when I was home. I had decided I would no longer put up with the dysfunction.

In June of 1988, I graduated from high school. Youth Group was ending, and I was on my own. I was offered to help coach volleyball the next season, and I gladly accepted their offer. I enjoyed it, but I wanted to be playing. Now I was in the real world of work, and it definitely was not the same.

I concentrated on work and going to school Monday through Friday, and I had the weekends off, which was perfect. I spent as much time as possible with the other family, even though I knew it would at some point all have to come to an end.

Chapter Three

Defining My Independence

My father and mother had always said that once you graduate from high school, or you turn 18, you will be out of the house and out on your own. I never questioned that, because I did not want to be there anyway. The strange thing is, my brothers stayed at home until one of my older brothers was twenty years old. My brother with schizophrenia never left home until later in life.

My contact with the four girls from my mother's church was pretty much nonexistent, now that the oldest girl was still a senior in high school.

I put all my heart, soul, time, and energy into working. I continued working at the pizza parlor, became full-time, and then I obtained a second job at a fast-food restaurant full-time. I was working 8:00 a.m.–4:30 p.m. at the fast-food restaurant, and 5:00 p.m.–1:00 a.m. at the pizza parlor, with alternate days off. My brain at this time was always racing. I did not realizesince I had not been diagnosed as of yet—that I was in a hypomanic state. I had no control. All I could think about was leaving home, getting out, and going somewhere far away, and I did not care how much or how hard I had to work for it. People at my jobs thought I was crazy. I thought they were crazy for not trying to better their lives and move ahead faster.

Thankfully an offer came from a friend I had in San Diego, California, whom I had met at one of the Youth Group's summer camps. I had met her at a camp in Texas when I was 17, and we had become great friends. I taught tennis there to younger campers and thoroughly enjoyed it. After my graduation from high school, she and her family invited me to move down to San Diego and live with them. My friend and I planned to live with her parents until we saved up enough money to get an apartment. At the pizza parlor and fast-food restaurants, I started earning as much money as possible to cover at least three months' expenses. That would be paying her parents rent for three months plus food.

I cannot remember the exact date I left for San Diego, but it was some time at the end of 1988. I did not have much difficulty finding a job down there. I started working for a medical supply company. It was so exciting and amazing to live in San Diego. There was so much to do in such a big city—not like the town I'd come from, with a population of only about 20,000.

Unfortunately, I did not last very long in San Diego. Since I was still somewhat of an introvert, life became too fast for me. I went to too many parties where I was uncomfortable; and we were going to Tijuana, where the drinking age was 18. That was my first time drinking, and I became very sick, which was not fun for me. My friend and I were not getting along. I was starting to build up resentments, and soon I saw that it was time to go back to Oregon. Sadly, I also left a young man I'd grown to love.

When I arrived back in Oregon, I had lost 15 pounds due to the stress I had put myself under down there. I went to the doctor to find out what was wrong with me. *Why was I losing so much weight?* I was 5'6", and weighed only 105 pounds. I was very upset when I went in to the doctor's office. The nurse took me back and weighed me. She looked at me sternly, and asked, "Are you trying to be anorexic, or is this just happening?" She really upset me. I went in to see the doctor, and he told me my problem was stress and pushing myself too hard. He gave me Zantac so my stomach would not ache, so I would eat. He then told me to rest for a few days. At this point, there were so many symptoms of bipolar in my life that were not recognized yet.

Back home, I had to stay with my father and mother for a while. To my surprise, they had turned my bedroom into a bigger living room. I had been away only a couple of months. That made me realize once again how hard and unloving my parents were. They knew I was having difficulties down in San Diego, and yet they removed my room anyway, which my brother was now using. I again felt unloved, and definitely unwanted. I slept on the couch, until I could move out.

I was offered back both of my jobs, and so I just started focusing on work as much as possible. I became obsessed with money, with becoming the best employee I could be, and with getting out of my parents' house. I knew working like this was my only escape, my only way to stay sane and have some control over my life.

Chapter Four

Something to Believe in: From Misery to Hope

After I left California, and also left the man I'd thought I was going to marry, I was very down. A lot was happening now. I was working the two full-time jobs again, and I was looking for a place I could call home. At the fast-food restaurant, I met Nina, who soon became my best friend. We were inseparable. We would find a party somewhere every night off I had, or after I was off of work. Parties were just getting started sometimes at 1:00 a.m.; or, we would cruise our small town. Cruising was the big thing to do. It was virtually the only thing to do really late at night, until the police stopped us from doing it.

I also met my future husband at the pizza place. I started noticing this same very nice-looking guy come in almost every night when I was working. He usually had one or two friends with him. There were two counter girls who worked with me at night. Rumors surfaced. They came to me and said, "There is someone who comes in all the time, who really likes you." With my low self-esteem, I guessed it was the most undesirable person I saw there regularly. My first reaction was that they were teasing me, and so I replied, "Who? The man who sleeps under the bridge, and comes in every day for free coffee?" But I was wrong. I was very surprised when they told me who this person was. It was the nice-looking man I had been noticing. He was very shy, and for over a month of coming in all the time, he never asked me out on a date, even though I had helped him at the counter several times.

One night I asked Nina to come in at the time I knew he would be there. She was very outgoing, so if he wanted a date, she would be the one to find out. She and I sat down at a table, and I saw his friends nudging him to come over. But then all four of them up and left. Nina said to me, "Let's follow them." We found them at the gas station. There was only one in town, where I traveled 14 miles each day there and back to work. Nina recognized one of his friends in the car, so they began talking and she asked where they were going. They said they were going up to Agate Lake, which was fairly nearby. It was frozen over this time of year, and there were never any police around. Finally that night, he asked me out. We saw each other every night after that. We were married four months later. Nina was my maid of honor. Twenty-seven years later, Nina and I are still the best of friends.

After my husband and I were married, we moved to Sacramento, California to be near his brother. He started a job with the construction company where his brother worked, which definitely did not turn out the way we expected. He was making only $8.00 an hour. We had been making three times this amount back home, so we were barely surviving. It was a nightmare. I had never been in this position in my life. My husband and I were arguing every day, because we were not able to pay our bills. I built up a huge resentment towards his brother. I felt set up. We had a good income and a positive future back in Oregon.

Thankfully, we moved back to Oregon. I went back to the fast-food restaurant, and they promoted me, and gave me health benefits as well. Since Sacramento put such a financial strain on us, we had to move in with my husband's parents for a few months to save up first and last months' rent for an apartment. He had to find a new job, and we needed to catch up.

I was so happy to be back in Oregon, to see Nina again, and to have my job back. Nina was still working at the fast-food restaurant, which made it even better to be back. One evening after work, Nina and I went to a party. My oldest brother—the one six years older— saw Nina for the first time, and was instantly attracted to her. They started dating. My brother was going through a divorce at the time. Finally the divorce was final and my brother and Nina were married. My husband and brother were good friends as well, so the four of us started hanging out and spending a lot of time together. It was wonderful. My husband and I had found a duplex to live in, and Nina and my brother found one right behind us. It was perfect. We could just hop the fence or walk around the corner to get to each other's duplex. I finally felt like my life was becoming manageable. I didn't have to think about the horrors of my parents' home.

After about two years my brother decided he wanted to be a corrections officer for the state of California. He went through their boot camp, and he and Nina moved to eastern California. I was pretty sad, but I knew I would still see them. This now started a new chapter in my life: I had a loving husband and a place to call home.

Chapter Five

Hallucinations and Obsessions

I was working and making plans for the future. My obsessiveness about the future was not setting well with me. I was putting so much pressure on myself to perform perfectly. One evening I experienced my first very scary hallucination. It would become one of many. As I was sleeping that night, I awoke to a very dark figure. It did not have a face, but it was coming down upon me from the ceiling and getting closer and closer. I was terrified. When it was about 12 inches from my face, I shouted at my husband. He awoke and assured me there was not anything there. For the first time I wondered if that was some craziness in my own mind, since he had not seen anything. I went back to sleep; but even now, 24 years later, I still have not forgotten the fear I had that night.

I wrote off in my mind what had happened that dark evening. I went back to work, and my obsessions with work continued. The obsessions would not go away, and I actually wasn't asking them to go. I seemed to thrive on my obsessions. My husband and I were both working. I was still the manager at the fast-food restaurant, and I became extremely obsessed with money—making money for myself, and making money for the restaurant. My motto was always *The harder you work, the luckier you become.* I had to work harder and harder to make more money, and the luck would come. Then, I figured, all the worries of the world would slip away.

CR

I decided I had a goal: I wanted a new home at age 25, and a baby. In February of 1995, we moved into our brand-new home, and I was pregnant. While I was pregnant with our daughter, my mother and father were living three hours away in Albany, Oregon. My father was transferred there after the mill he was working at in our hometown burnt down. For a completely unknown reason to me, I decided that I wanted my mother to be with me after my baby was born. She also wanted to be there with me.

The day arrived, and I went into labor. I had given my husband very strict instructions not to let my mother in the room during labor and delivery. I wasn't sure why. I just knew I felt very vulnerable and uncomfortable around her. I was still harboring some deep resentments against her. However, after pushing for four and a half hours, I asked my husband to go get her. In that delivery room, I actually saw her shed a tear.

Later, it shocked me that I changed my mind and asked her to come in. I realized that no matter how much I may have hated her in the past, I still wanted her to prove to me that she loved me and cared. I admit, though, that this was not a good feeling. I felt weak for having asked her to be in there. I was always on my own, and I never wanted to depend on her for anything.

She actually did prove herself to be very helpful that week following my daughter's birth. She helped out with cooking, and showed me how to give my daughter her first bath. I did appreciate that. She was showing things to me with my daughter that I never thought she was capable of: love, nurturing, and joy. Perhaps she may have been like that with me as a baby, I don't know. I doubt it; not with two other children living in the home. I was probably never given the care she was showing for my daughter. After my mother left, I stayed at home for six weeks, and then went back to work. My energy level every day was too high to be able to stay home; and I couldn't ignore my drive for work and money. Thank God, I found a wonderful nanny. This allowed me to come home in the evenings and be the mother I wanted to be.

My life from there went right back to obsession and creativity. Every evening, I would wake up in the middle of the night. I would awaken with swarming thoughts in my mind, never knowing that these racings thoughts were part of a much bigger picture that I would soon discover. During the night, I would awaken with thought after thought of different ways to improve everything I was doing. I kept a notebook beside my bed so I could write them down. I would then take them to work with me and start putting them into action.

ɔᴙ

It was time to break new ground. Now I was 28, and I quit the fast-food business and went to work for a collections agency. It offered much better pay and benefits. I had been looking for something different; the restaurant business was all I had known for almost 11 years. Working at the collections agency was not rewarding at all mentally. Hounding people for money was not the person I wanted to be. But I was glad to be doing something new.

Unfortunately, one day, while I was at work, I received a phone call that my grandmother had had a heart attack. I was horrified. I said to myself, *If she dies, I die too.* I didn't know that this was to be another symptom to the beginning of bipolar disorder. I started having a major anxiety attack before I was even out of the building. I thought I was having a heart attack. I had chest pain and trouble breathing.

That evening, after I saw my grandmother, I went to the doctor, knowing that for sure in my mind I was having—or had already had—a heart attack. She knew by my age and health that it was not true. She told me so, and said she wanted to put me on a type of experimental anti-anxiety medication that had just come out at the time, called Buspar, and I said no. So she gave me a prescription for Xanax instead, and I felt fine about that. I kept the Xanax with me every day, and would take it pretty consistently. It did not make me groggy or sleepy. It helped me to do my job better and be more relaxed all day, since I tended to be extremely high-strung.

Instead of obsessing so much about money, I started obsessing over my grandmother. I was constantly making sure she was eating like she was supposed to, and making her dinners when I could. My mother was three hours away, so I felt I was the only person that truly cared to help her eat right, and check in on her once a day.

ᘓ

When I had been with the collections agency for a year, I become pregnant with our second daughter. By this time my parents had moved back to our hometown. It was a rough birth with my second daughter, born in September, 1999. When she came into this world, she wasn't breathing. At the moment when they whisked her away from me, I panicked until I could see her, which wasn't for several hours. It turned out that she had several problems when she was born, and spent five days in neonatal Intensive Care. (Today she is in perfect health.) Again, at that time of the birth of my child, I saw some true colors come out in my mother: She was surprisingly helpful to have around.

After our second daughter was born, I wanted some way of making a little extra money, so I began helping my mother with her house-cleaning business, a day or two a week. While helping her on a new home construction cleaning job, I found out that the contractor who built the home was looking for an office manager. I did not have a whole lot of experience with computers, but he hired me anyway. It started out as a part-time job, and then about six months later, I went to full-time. I thoroughly enjoyed learning about the ins and outs of construction, and all the building phases of a home. I saw how the financing worked as well, with both private lenders and conventional ones.

My next step became getting my license to become a loan officer, and to do all of the in-house loans. I started doing loans for other people as well. Doing home loans was very gratifying. It gave me the opportunity to fulfill people's dreams of owning a home. Later in the construction part of the business, I was given a new truck, and I was made project manager for the company. It was now the year 2002. Being the project manager did a lot for my self-esteem. I was very good at completing the homes on time. Nevertheless, I began obsessing over them at night, and again making numerous notes to myself.

During the time I was the project manager, my husband and I were having some marital issues. He agreed to go to counseling. The first time we met with the therapist, she was asking about our backgrounds, and decided she needed to see me on a one-on-one basis for a while before he ought to come back in. She was mainly focusing on the molestation that happened in my childhood. She was the first professional to give me a diagnosis: Post-Traumatic Stress Disorder (PTSD). I have been in therapy ever since then. I stayed with that particular therapist from 2002 until 2007.

Chapter Six

Holding onto Hope through the Pain

I was still working for the construction company when I got the news: My father had been taken to the emergency room for a blockage in his colon. They removed the blockage and said he wouldn't live long, maybe until Christmas. This was in September. I was devastated, and furious with the doctor. He was the most insensitive doctor I had encountered in my life. Later, my father was diagnosed with neuro-endocrine cancer, an incurable cancer. He was 57. We were told he could go into remission, but that he would never be able to beat this disease.

I went crazy again. My mind never goes to thinking about me. It dwells instead on making everyone else better. This is *one-way thinking*, a symptom of bipolar disorder. My father fought with everything he had, and did indeed go into remission. Unfortunately, this remission only lasted for 13 months. No matter what my father was, or what he had done, he was still my father—good, bad, or ugly. I could not escape that. His illness drastically changed me. I became the doting daughter. I think back now, and ask myself why. *Why didn't I leave that up to my mother?* Did I not trust her? Or was I just sick? I was still seeing a therapist, who really was not of that much help. My mind was too focused on my work and on my father—not on what illness I myself might have.

During the time period of my father's illness, I tried to go on with business as usual. I had decided to go into business for myself.

I started a construction company. By this time I knew all about the construction business and the financing, so there was no reason for me not to do it. I had a passion for both trades. I started selling houses so quickly I could barely keep up. Demand was extremely high in the area where I lived. All this activity did not stop me from thinking about my father every day.

My therapist, knowing what I would ultimately be facing, referred me to a psychologist in Tennessee. He specialized in Intensive Integrative Relational Therapy. So I went to Tennessee. This was quite a break. When I arrived, they had an apartment for me to stay in, for a one-week session, 9:00 to 5:00 every day. It was by far the best week I have ever had with a psychologist. I was there to prepare for my father's death and another to come. He was able to bring things out in me that had been suppressed for many years. The psychologist and I became very close, and I had thoughts about buying a home there. I even put $10,000 dollars down on one. I had great admiration for this man and started to learn a little about him and his wonderful family. He is not practicing any longer, but has written several books. His name is Dr. Don Doyle, and you can find him and his books on the internet. They are a very easy read, and I would highly recommend them.

After Tennessee, I arrived home to some news about my father. My father's remission ended in 2004, and they gave him four to six months to live. I was trying so hard to keep it together mentally and emotionally as I was facing the death of my father. My children, who were only three and seven, would be losing their grandfather. I was devastated at the thought of his death.

By my own initiation, my father and I had started cultivating a relationship. Surprisingly, it had been coming along well. He was a wonderful grandfather to my children, and now it seemed I had started to matter in his life. But now I was going to lose him. I would never be able to forget the past. I started becoming very anxious and depressed. My father's cancer remained at the forefront of my mind. It was turning my world upside down. I was having a hard time holding the business and myself together.

I started seeing a nurse practitioner. I was explaining to her how I was feeling: anxious, depressed, and angry. Out of the blue, the nurse practitioner said, "I think you have bipolar."

Immediately, I flared up. "I cannot honestly believe you are saying this to me! You know what I am going through, and you chalk it up to bipolar!" I refused her medication, and left. I was in total disbelief and denial.

This would not be the last time that I would hear a doctor tell me this. I was extra defensive, because I felt that she was saying I was a failure, and that my life and career were over. Her timing was also the absolute worst.

Chapter Seven

How I Coped with Tragedy

Now that I had a very successful business, I was making a lot of money. I went to my father after he was given the three to six months to live, and asked him, "If you could go anywhere in the world, where would you like to go?"

He responded, "Hawaii." So I spent $12,000 to take him there. Other people thought I was crazy. They did not understand my reasoning. Honestly, I did not know why I was spending the money and taking him there. Even my mother kept telling me it was frivolous; however, I was absolutely adamant about it. Nothing was going to stop me.

Right away, I booked tickets for my mother, father, brother, niece, my husband, children, and myself. We stayed in Hawaii for seven days. My father was amazed at the beauty. My husband and I had been to Hawaii two times before, so we already knew the best resort. I am so happy I was able to fulfill my father's heart's desire to see Hawaii. However, I did ask myself: *Was this his heart's desire, or mine?* With the madness, depression, and anxiety that come along with my disease, it was impossible for me to discern what was true. Our trip was fun for my family, but I did wonder how much fun my father was having. My moods were up and down. I went from depressed to elated during the entire trip. I was not able to tell what he was thinking or feeling.

While at the resort in Maui, I asked my father if he would like to go to Pearl Harbor, and he did not hesitate to say yes. My husband, my father, and I flew to Pearl Harbor from Maui. We had a wonderful day there. I was fascinated, and my husband and father as well were captivated. I became a little disheartened when my father could not go inside the ships, as his lungs were failing and he could not make it up all of the stairs. Overall, the fact that I could see how much joy he was experiencing was priceless.

When we went back to Maui, my father enjoyed the resort's two-and-a-half–acre pool with its beautiful waterfall. He was so brave to go swimming; he had lost all of his hair now, and was very noticeably ill. Later, we would go back to our rooms, and when I saw him with his cap and shirt off, I became so sad I would start crying and have to go into my room. He stayed so absolutely strong; but my heart was breaking. Nevertheless, whenever we were swimming in the ocean or pools, I fully realized that for the first time in my life I was seeing my father happy, joyous, and free. I am extremely grateful for that time, and for the fact that God provided the money to make it happen.

The trip was coming to an end and I had been holding back a lot of emotion while there. I knew I was going to have to cope with the death of my father, sooner or later, after we arrived home. Now I remember that back while I was scheduling the trip, I was very delusional. My thinking was one way and one way only— black and white, with no variables—a common symptom of bipolar disorder with psychotic features. I was actually feeling like I owed him something. No one could talk me out of planning it. The reality was, *he* owed *me* for the 18 years of pain and misery he had caused as I grew up. My mind was choosing at the time to overlook it all, to ignore the fact that he had never acknowledged his behavior nor apologized for it.

Through therapy, I learned that my father's behavior was not normal, and that the way I had to exist was not normal. Unbelievably, for some reason this came as a surprise to me. I really don't know how it could be that I often called my home "the realms of hell," and yet after I was away awhile, I ended up ignoring and trying to forget all the pain I endured. I was trying to ignore my heart, and I kept it well-guarded. I was putting more time and energy into his life, so that I could forget about mine—both my past and my future. I was making him out to be the saint, with me as the sinner. Believe it or not, this is the way I coped. I still loved him dearly, but therapy certainly opened my eyes to the fact that I had lived a miserable existence.

I still do suffer from the past due to my traumatic childhood home environment. But now, I have chosen to forgive. To forgive is not to forget, but forgiveness is still the right thing to do. Forgiveness helps the heart to heal.

Chapter Eight

Home Again—and Looking to the Future

When we arrived home from Maui, my father was into his second month of the three-to-six–month prediction. A hospice worker started coming out every Friday. My mother was in denial about my father's impending death, so she would ask me to stay with Dad whenever the hospice worker came out. I told her I would. She would go to work, and I would be the one to get the bad news from hospice care. Her leaving like this and using me as a scapegoat was typical of her. I was 33 years old at the time, and she was constantly taking advantage of how big my heart was. I did end up caring for my father several days each week. Later, she would throw me to the wolves when I would tell her what news hospice care had that day. I would try to explain, but she would just accuse me of not having faith. This of course was a ridiculous statement. I now understand. He was her one-and-only true love for 40 years, and she couldn't deal with him leaving.

My mother and father owned some property at the beach with my uncle. My uncle would spend his summers at the Oregon coast, and his winters in Arizona. This was always my father's dream for when he retired. My father's desire to spend time at the beach became very strong. They had previously sold their recreational vehicle; so now they needed something to stay in if they were to go to the beach, since their property was bare land.

My husband and I had just purchased a travel trailer, so we offered it to my parents to live in while at their property. We pulled it over to the beach for them, and they would stay there four days a week. Then they'd come home on Thursdays for hospice care, which came on Fridays, and my mother would go off to work. This continued until October. Then it was time to bring the RV home because the weather was changing at the beach. It was becoming too cold by that time, and my father's health was declining further. While my father had been spending all this time at the coast, my husband, our children, and I had spent as much time as we could going over there to be with him.

ఐ

My father was becoming weaker and weaker. After arriving back home, he declared a great desire to go to Arizona one last time. He was relentless. He wanted to take our truck and travel trailer on the one-thousand–mile trip. Against our wishes, and against the advice of hospice care, he and my mother left. At this time, my father's body was succumbing to the disease very quickly. We were extremely worried about him making this trip. Not only were we concerned about his welfare, but also we were worried about my mother's safety, since he was driving. It took them four days to get there. It is typically a two-day trip, but he stopped and slept about every four hours. They finally arrived—only to have to turn back five days later. My father's condition had become extremely critical. He had to lift his own legs into the truck. My husband and I wanted to go meet them, but my father refused. He said he drove the truck down there, and he was going to drive it back. It took them six days to get home. He had to stop very frequently to lie down and sleep, because he was in a lot of pain.

Back home again, my father was at the end of his life. He and I sat in his garage together one last time, looking out over the view.

He finally talked to me the way I had always wished he would have done when I was growing up: very tender and loving.

☓

At that point, it was time to call my oldest brother and let him know that my father's death was fast approaching. After my brother arrived, my father had two more good days in his recliner. The hospice worker was there every day now. He was moved to a hospital bed. He was in constant pain. My mother and brother took care of his personal needs, and I would talk with hospice care to take care of his medications for anxiety and pain.

My own anxiety level was very high. I was taking Xanax and getting by as best I could.

I had so many questions for my father, and since he was at the end of his journey, I really wanted to ask. He could barely speak, but I managed to ask him the question that most haunted and taunted me: "Dad?" I asked. "Do you believe in heaven?"

He answered, "One-hundred percent," and held my hand. It was the last time he spoke.

He passed away the following day, November 11, 2004. He had just turned 60 years old. I was 34. I felt robbed of time. Death is a horrible thing to witness especially when it's your own father.

☓

My mother was never interested in another man again. For me, my father's death seemed to throw me into another dimension of my life. It felt like the beginning of the end to me. I hid my emotions from everyone. I have been told that bipolar individuals are very good at stuffing emotions and suffering in silence. That is certainly what was happening to me. It is very painful to stuff feelings, when you really need to let them out.

Chapter Nine

My Immense Pain and Suffering

I was trying to avoid my thoughts of all those wasted years of my father's absence and abuse, yet instead I became obsessed with these thoughts. He was gone. That was it. I went back to work, trying to run my business successfully. I don't know how I had maintained the business at this horrible time. My mother was becoming very needy. My parents owned two RV parks, and two homes. Before my father died, he had tried to show my mother how to do the bookkeeping, but she had refused to listen. She had stayed in denial about his impending death. Now that he was gone, whom did she always run to when she was needy? Me. And then she'd throw me away.

Now she needed me to do all of her bookkeeping for her. I would go home at night after running my own business, and then do the bookkeeping for her and pay all of her bills. I became extremely overloaded and stressed. Once more, stress and chaos were back in my life and trying to overrun it.

I was still in shock over the loss of my father. Little by little, I grew weak, tired, and emotionally unstable. I did not know what was happening. I was told I was creeping into a serious deep depression. All I felt was doom and gloom. Watching my father's death had been surreal. I was not afraid to die, but I soon realized that I was in the most miserable state of mind I had ever been in. I finally admitted something was wrong. I called the psychiatric nurse practitioner and scheduled an appointment. It seemed as if it took forever to get in to see her. I told her I was miserable because my father had just passed, and I needed medications to get me through. I wanted something for anxiety and sleep. She prescribed Trazodone, Xanax, and Depakote. I had no idea what Depakote was. I took the pills—all except for the Trazodone—before I left her office. I ended up in the middle of nowhere, with no idea how to get home. I called my therapist in Tennessee—my good friend Don—and told him what was happening to me. I had OnStar in my vehicle, and he suggested I try that. I did, and I made it home. I never took another dose of Depakote again.

I was still extremely overwhelmed the following day. I attempted to overdose on the Trazodone. Since it was prescribed for sleep, I thought I would just go to sleep and not wake up. All Trazodone did for me was give me a horrible headache. It was not like any other headache I had experienced. I had to call for help, and my mother came. She took me to the psychiatric unit in a hospital located 26 miles away. I was admitted for two days. After the two days were up, my mother came to get me. On the way home, for the first time ever, I set a boundary with her. I told her I would no longer do her bookkeeping; it was too much.

CR

In the psychiatric hospital where I spent those two days, I was told that I had Bipolar 1 Disorder. The psychiatric nurse practitioner confirmed it, too. I did not want to fight the diagnosis anymore. I just wanted help. Now I had to face the reality of it.

CR

I was no longer doing my mother's bookkeeping, and this helped me to realize that I had been so busy with everything else, I was still in shock over my father's death. Because of all the responsibilities, I had not been given the opportunity to miss him. I started to question everything all over again. Was heaven real? I was not emotionally stable, so these thoughts of wondering where he had gone were haunting me.

Now I was serious, and wanting answers. I could not keep feeling this way. Some people can journey on through life and death, and accept that it is just a process. Maybe so! Not for me. I was going to try my best to find out the truth. My mother's religion spoke only of hell and judgment day. I was determined to find the correct answer for my own peace and sanity.

Chapter Ten

First Hypomanic Episode

It had been two months now since my father had passed. That desire for answers from God was inevitable now. I wanted either a *yes* or a *no*. I knew I was acting a little crazy. I could see that I was emotionally unstable due to the misery and unanswered questions about his death. One night, I was completely out of my mind, and extreme madness took over. I no longer felt like me. I had never felt this way before. My mind was racing in circles, and I could not stop the spinning and spinning. It just kept going, and I had to go with it. My concentration was absent completely. I took off to the beach where my parents' property had been. I was looking for answers, I suppose. I drove up to the top of the parking area to look out at the ocean. Then I took off out of the car, running down to the beach. It was 1:00 a.m., raining and freezing, and I ran three feet out into the water, yelling at God.

I would run for a while, then stop, and then shout out at God, asking, *"Where is he? If he is alive in heaven or somewhere, why can't you show me? It is so easy for you!"*

Each time, I would run about a quarter-mile, and stop and shout again at God. The next time when I stopped, I looked out, and a seal popped up, staring at me. I thought, *What is this?* I said to God, "Come *on*! Is this supposed to be a sign?"

I took off running again, ran approximately another quarter-mile, and then stopped to look out again. There was that same seal, just staring at me intently. I could actually look into its eyes. I was still questioning God, but I was also coming to my senses a little, seeing the craziness of my thinking and actions. I suddenly realized that my vehicle was parked in the worst possible place, so I ran as fast as I could back to my car.

As I turned to go up the bank, I stopped and looked out upon the ocean, and there was the seal again! *That seal was following me back to safety.*

We certainly cannot explain some things in life. I choose now to believe that my father's spirit was with me in that seal.

Chapter Eleven

Hospitals

After my hypomanic experience, I became extremely depressed. I had not experienced very much deep depression in the past, so when it came on I was stunned. It hit me like a ton of bricks—a brick wall so high and so thick, there was no way out. I was terrified. I did not have any energy. Walking was a chore. My dreams were crumbling down around me. Bipolar disorder had now taken over my life completely. It was dark, ugly, and miserable; and I was nothing but misery to others. I experienced hallucinations and delusions. I was empty inside, and very lonely. I tried to keep working and keep up with my responsibilities, but I was just not capable of managing. I tried to keep both my construction business and my finances going. It was not possible.

On the weekends when my daughters were out of school, we had always gone somewhere as a family. Now, I did not have any interest in life or even in leaving my home anymore. I contemplated suicide so many times. Thank God, I did not follow through. On weekends my husband would take the girls out and do grocery shopping, or do something fun with them. They were only four and seven at this time. I felt of no use or value to them, which only deepened my depression.

There were only a handful of psychiatrists in our small town, and unfortunately I was stuck with the one I disliked the most. The medications he was giving me were not working. At work, homeowners for whom I was building homes insisted upon seeing me, to go over their wish lists—understandably so. I could not hide out at my home office on those days. I would get myself into the office somehow, but I was in a terrible mood. Somehow, when it came to my clients, I was always able to put a smile on my face.

After attempting to keep my brave face for several months, I knew I had to go somewhere to get help. I wanted to go to a non-lockdown facility, where I would have some freedom to walk outside in nature. After all, nature is what I grew up in, and what made the most sense to me since I was a small child.

After searching the Internet, I found Harvard's McLean Hospital in Boston, Massachusetts, a psychiatric facility. Apart from the big McLean Hospital itself, they had a private home on campus with approximately 12 rooms. Harvard was a long way from home, but I was desperate for the best help I could get, which settled my decision. Staying alive was better than committing suicide out of severe anguish and pain. I knew I had to be proactive and find a hospital that actually offered the possibilities and professionals to change my life and give me the stability I so desperately longed for. McLean had all the psychiatric facilities and opportunities right there on one campus, where all my needs could be met.

CR

Before I left for Harvard, my mother offered to help me financially. It shocked me that she realized I needed that kind of help, since she had not recognized my disease at any other time thus far. She offered a substantial amount, equal to a quarter of the cost of my stay. It was amazing to have any offer at all from her. Once arriving back at home for good from Harvard, I mentioned the money she had promised me. She responded, "Weren't you able to cover the hospital expenses yourself?" I answered her truthfully: yes. Yet her help would have shown to me some love and recognition of my disease, which I so desperately desired from her. She withdrew her offer of money, and I was not surprised.

This private home at Harvard with all my medical needs had been very expensive, and it did put a strain on me financially. However, it was all worth it. I had a private room, with my own bathroom and access to laundry; it was not at all like a hospital. I thank God I had worked as much as I had, and therefore I was able to afford to go there for seclusion and treatment.

To my surprise, they even had a van, which any patient could use, if desired, to go into the city, where they would let us walk around in the small shops. Big stores were off limits because they had to keep track of where we all were. Near the end of our time in town, we would hang out at Starbucks for a bit. Being in the city made me feel like a normal citizen, living a normal life. What a breath of fresh air were these days in the city.

One weekend at McLean, I had made a special request, just for myself. It sounds odd to some, I am sure. I had never seen the ocean on the east coast, so I asked if someone would drive me to the beach to see the difference in water, air, sand, noise—anything that might heighten my senses and improve my state of mind. Being in nature and especially the ocean—that is where my peace temporarily came from as a child, and as an adult, too, before the depression took over.

I did not expect them to approve it, but they did. I was even able to go by myself, with just one of the counselors. I was so amazed at the difference between the Atlantic Ocean and the Pacific. Waves of the Pacific are high, and I'd rarely seen any surfers; the sand is grey and rocky. At the Atlantic Ocean, I was taken aback by the brownish color of the sand, and small waves, even though it was stormy the day I visited. It was a wonderful treat, which I will surely never forget. I went so far as to bring back a small bottle of the sand. Today it is still tan-colored.

CR

In the psychiatric facility there were nurses and counselors on staff 24 hours a day. During the day, I would meet with psychologists, therapists, social workers, and psychiatrists, as well as a psychopharmacologist. I didn't see every one of them every day, but at least several each day. They did extensive testing on my brain, performed CAT scans and EEGs, tested me with Rorschach cards, and more. I will never understand the significance of those cards. They are just blobs to me.

After I settled in, they immediately started trying medications. I saw two psychiatrists. One believed I had schizophrenia, since there was such a strong history of the disease in my family. I knew that was not possible because I already knew first-hand what the disease looked like. He dropped that diagnosis fairly quickly. All of the different medications we tried were not working to bring me out of my depression. I was on a lot of medications, and in no time at all I had gained 25 pounds. Fortunately, after I was back home, I did lose the weight.

Since the medications were not working, they eventually wanted to try ECT (electro-convulsive therapy). At first, I said *no way*, because ECT is what they had done to my uncle when he was locked up for 32 years. They eventually convinced me that it was extremely effective in treating depression, so I agreed to try it.

Their plan was to put me through a series of treatments, until they decided the depression was getting better. Then they would keep going, until they reached a certain number that they had set in their mind. They wanted 11 total. There are a lot of different opinions about ECT; but the truth is, I can only tell what it felt like for me. One of the most worrying parts of ECT is that it is not a cure. Once I was home, they said I would have to have maintenance ECTs three times a week for the first two weeks, and then keep going until the doctors wished to stop, as they would determine if I were better. To do these maintenance ECTs from where I lived, I would have had to drive either four hours north, or five hours south, to go to hospitals where they performed them.

CR

Once I made up my mind to do it, I kept telling myself that Jesus and God's angels would be right beside me.

The nurses would come and wake me up at 6:00 a.m., and take me down to the actual hospital to have the treatment. They put me into a hospital bed, and hooked me up to an EKG machine. Then they would take me into the ECT room, and show me the device they were going to use. They would put some gel on my head, where they were going to place the device. Their goal was for me to have the best possible seizure.

Afterwards, I would wake up in a recovery room, with several other people who also had just had the ECT done. Their practice at the hospital was that after each person, the next would go right in. I would see about 10 people waking up in the recovery room at the same time as I was. After ten minutes or so, they would take five or so of us to another room where we waited in chairs, and had orange juice and English muffins. A little while later, the doctor would call me in and tell me how my seizure went. Not what I wanted to hear. I felt like I was being herded like cattle. It was the most frightening experience I have ever had in my life. When I awoke, my brain was completely empty. I did not recognize anything. It was like I was from another planet. ECT literally erases your mind for a few minutes. Eventually, you come out of it, and remember what just happened. When you wake up, it is like having to put a puzzle together all over again for about 30 minutes—a puzzle of people, places, and things: my *life*.

While I was going through those first ECT treatments, I asked my husband to fly to Massachusetts, so that he could be with me when I would awaken. A familiar face made me recall things faster. He always stood right beside me when I needed him. My mind was so crazy at the time, as soon as he arrived, I would ask him to leave. I don't know why I acted that way. Was it craziness? Or did I just not want him to see me that way? Anyway, for future treatments I started asking one of the nurses in my building to be there when I awoke. After four treatments, I told the doctors no more. They were not helping. Maybe I did not give them a chance, maybe I should have had 11 as they wanted, but my gut said no. For me, they were demoralizing, humiliating, and inhumane. Although I do know people with bipolar who have had success with ECT, the experience was too disconcerting.

While at the hospital, I found out that my oldest daughter had made it to a State Choir Competition, and I wanted to be there. I told the social worker I wanted to go home for a few days to attend the competition. She was reluctant. I went home anyway, and during the time I was home I went out of my mind again, with madness and craziness. I was still not well.

One evening I became very aggressive and unreasonable, and punched a hole in the wall. It just came on instantly. In my case, madness, and rage usually do come on in an instant. Sometimes, even when I am stable, it can come on for a moment, and then leave fairly soon after. After I punched the hole in the wall, I started to leave in my car to go down to the bar. My husband jerked some wires out so I could not drive. I was so furious, I told him that he would never be able to stop me from doing something I was set on doing. I started to run, sprinting towards the bar. It was about two miles from my home. He started looking for me, but I was running and dodging in and out of fences. I did not know he had called my mother and brother to help find me. They did finally find me, behind the corner of a fence. I climbed up into my brother's truck. They started talking to me, and I calmed down. They eventually convinced me to go home, take my Seroquel, and go to sleep.

The next morning, it was time to go back to Harvard. When I arrived back at the hospital, the social worker who had released me to go home had already been informed by my husband of what had happened at home. She was not pleased. She asked me if I thought she should have committed me to the main hospital before I left. I replied that I did not know; maybe so. I realized that my behavior was not normal, and my daughters once again had witnessed my madness.

I knew I was a very sick person, needing desperately to get well. The next day, I met with the psychopharmacologist. Even though I had said no to any more ECTs, the doctor continued to try to push them on me, but I just could not stand the thought of having more. He finally agreed, and started adding new medications, plus therapy and coping classes to my routine, such as DBT (dialectical behavioral therapy) and cognitive behavioral therapy. All the patients at the hospital were unique, and each person had different needs. Some classes fit the needs of some people better than others. After staying there for two and a half months, I came home. I was not completely stable, but I was a lot more stable than I had been.

Chapter Twelve

Mania

There was not anything pleasant about being home again, except for seeing my children. My husband and I went back to what we'd been doing before: arguing and yelling. Our relationship was not there anymore, so we decided to get a divorce. Beforehand, we had tried everything. We took a trip to Tahiti, just the two of us, which was a fabulous trip. But once we arrived back home, the reality of real life would come back. More fighting, arguing, and yelling. We attempted one other thing to bring us all back together: a Disney Cruise with our daughters. It was unbearable for me. I spent at least two hours a day in our room sleeping, and the rest of the day dragging myself around, depressed. I was not completely stable yet. I desired so wholeheartedly to be the perfect mother on the ship, but my illness did not allow it.

Luckily, my husband was all over the ship with the girls at all times. They went swimming, played at the arcade, and ate late-night ice cream bars. Watching him being able to do these things with them both enraged and saddened me. I cannot possibly explain how I felt. My little children must have felt that I did not want to participate in such a wonderful adventure. I wanted nothing more than to be able to be with them. I held a hatred for this disease that I would not shake easily. I was stricken with a horrible disease that I certainly did not ask for. I am fortunate that my children now know a lot about my disease, and can forgive me. Today they know that I have always adored them, but mentally I did not have the capacity to be who I longed to be—to be who they longed for me to be.

I want to make it clear that my decision to divorce was when I was of sound mind—that is, if you can call any real major decisions made by bipolar individuals *sound*. I always do go back and forth when I have to make tough decisions. I double- and triple-check, making sure to decipher the points over and over, asking, *Is this the bipolar Darcie? Or the stable of-sound-mind Darcie?*

I was stable at this time after coming home from Harvard, so this decision was clear to me. Our marriage before my bipolar diagnosis had already been tumultuous. It had been like that even before my father passed away. I had to protect my sanity by divorcing. It was very hard to do, because he was a good man, and a good father, and we both loved each other. Other people would tell us we were like oil and water: We didn't mix. Our marriage lasted 17 years. We fought with all we had to repair it. It was not fixable.

CR

Now I was facing the challenges of my business. It was failing and in ruin. Far beyond repair. Houses were not being completed on time, which was adding more and more to the building costs of the homes. I was helpless, and there was not anything I could do to stop it. No one knew how to run the financial part of the business while I had been in the hospital, so the business was tanking. I knew it was time to pull out. It was a devastating realization. I loved my work, and now I had to let everything go. Lose everything.

I started to feel like a failure. I had nothing left of my business, and my marriage and my mind were being destroyed. Due to my health insurance companies cancelling all of my policies, I no longer had any access to my medications. Mania was starting to creep in. There was not any one person in my family willing to pitch in to help me pay for my medications. Not even my own mother. When my father passed, she received a good amount of life insurance from him, so she was financially able to help me; but she chose not to help me. Just the Lithium and Seroquel would have helped.

All together, my four medications were $1000 per month. Lithium, though, was one of the less-expensive ones. At that time in Oregon, there was a waiting list which took anyone applying at least six months to one year to receive any kind of health insurance through the state. I was beside myself. I knew what was going to happen, and I could not do anything about it. Just a week or so later, I went to a support group. This is where I met a woman in a manic state as well. We became best of friends while both being in the same state of mind. We shared as well similar positions in life, with divorce and other trials.

We started going to the bars every night. We would get there at 7:00 p.m. or so, and stay until closing. We were severely manic. We became lost in our disease of madness, in a crazy world that would greatly take advantage of our state of mind. Our judgment was completely gone. We started bringing men to my home, where I had a large heated pool and hot tub. It was a constant party. If we did not all come home to my house, we would find a local motel somewhere.

I do remember hating what was going on, yet not seeing a way to stop it. I was on a rollercoaster that was never going to stop unless we found a way to get off. We both desperately wanted help, but no one would help us. Psychiatrists would not see us since we did not have any insurance and no income. This is where the system threw us under the bus. We tried on several occasions to advocate for ourselves, but no one listened or cared. Government programs threw us aside like we were trash and did not deserve help. We did not belong anywhere. Everyone in our lives had left us, and no one was willing to help.

I was so miserable, doing things that disgusted me; yet my mind was racing a million miles an hour and there seemed to be no other outlet except bars, alcohol, and men. At least the men would make me feel cared for, for a short period of time—until I felt used up. I did all these things beyond my control. The disease took away my ability to think, or to make any decent decisions. With my mind racing so quickly, I never knew where it might stop temporarily during the day, if at all. My existence was miserable, and full of torment.

In the face of bipolar, I tried immensely to figure out who Darcie was. I knew this person I was seeing in the mirror each day was not me, the intelligent one, nor the me who is the shy one and gravely ill. I was looking from the outside at a person I did not know: a woman who had never even been to a bar before the madness of bipolar took hold of her life. This life was bringing up a lot of shame and guilt. I saw my children very little during this time.

I remember taking my six-year-old daughter down the river on a rafting trip. She was terrified because the waves kept coming over the bow. I knew what I was doing, but she did not know that I did. She has never gone down the river with me since.

My oldest daughter was playing eighth-grade basketball that same year. I do not remember her playing at all. It breaks my heart. She tells me that I came to some of the games. My favorite sport was basketball, and yet I don't remember anything. I blame a lot of my memory loss on ECT. I was so sick from this disease, it shatters my heart inside, because I know I will never have these times back.

℞

After over a year of this madness and crazy life, I decided to commit suicide. I was very serious about ending my life, and ending all of the suffering in my children's and family's life. I wrote suicide letters to my daughters, to my ex-husband, to my mother, to my grandmother, and to my oldest brother. I placed them all neatly on the kitchen counter, went and got the bottle of Lithium that I had just bought, lay down on the living room floor, and took 27 300-milligram tablets. I started to feel sleepy, and my breathing became very shallow. I thought to myself, *If this is how I am going to die, please Lord just let me go.* It was not an unpleasant feeling at all.

My friend Samantha found me, and called an ambulance. I was not happy about it, but I did not fight them either. I knew that would have been a mistake. They could definitely make my life much worse than it already was going to be. When we arrived at the hospital, they started pumping me full of charcoal, which binds the Lithium up so that it stops traveling through your system.

After I was in the emergency for a little while and had become lucid, I started being questioned by different mental facilities. They were threatening to admit me to the same mental institution where my uncle had spent thirty two years. This terrified me. I had five days in the mental hospital they had currently placed me in to prove I was fit for society and that I was a fit parent.

I spent two days in that hospital. After they released me from the emergency room, they put me into a lockdown holding room, which was like a jail cell. There was a bed on the floor, and magazines. There was a door that remained open, but with an imaginary line they told me I was not allowed to cross. I could not believe this was my life that I was living. The humiliation was just never-ending. After the two days had passed, they transferred me in a disgusting car—with bars on the windows—to a psychiatric hospital 30 miles away. It is the only psychiatric hospital nearby. I saw a social worker while I was there two or three times, and eventually I was able to convince her that I would not try to commit suicide again. She believed me, and five days later I was released.

☙

This whole ordeal—about possibly losing my children and going to Mental Hospital—scared me to death. Thankfully, it put the fear of God in me. After all, He was the only One able to protect me from myself, from this disease, and from me taking my own life. God was the only one on my side, and He was all I needed. I am grateful now that I had such a strong belief in Him.

God found a way into my mother's heart. After she had witnessed the severity of my disease, she was now trying to help me to get back on medications, to seeing a psychiatric nurse practitioner and to finding a new therapist. Starting fresh with a new doctor and therapist was the best thing I could have done at that time. They both turned out to be exceptional, and very caring. They truly had compassion. I also joined a group called Celebrate Recovery. I was finally gaining some control of my life. I was starting to feel empowered spiritually and mentally again. Celebrate Recovery is a twelve-step spiritually based program that helps with many different obstacles an individual may be struggling with: They call them *hurts*, *habits*, and *hangups*. Working on past hurts, and looking at some of the other areas of my troubled life, was like having two therapists. The Celebrate Recovery program really helped me to become strong, and to realize that I have to deal with a grave disease. I did not ask for this disease, which can become all-consuming if I allow it to—by not taking my medication or by not doing the other self-care steps. A sure way *not* to survive this disease is to stop taking medication or to abuse alcohol and drugs—putting yourself in a lonely, horrible state of self-pity, and exposing yourself to the strong possibility of suicide. I chose instead to stay alive and sane.

Chapter Thirteen

Guilt and Remorse

After my manic episode and my suicide attempt, the mental anguish I felt was so deep, it seemed the darkness in my mind would never end. Even with my therapist, doctor, and Celebrate Recovery group, I was riddled with guilt. To say I felt horrible about what I did to my ex-husband, children, and the rest of my family during mania would be a huge understatement. I cannot imagine what was going through my children's minds when I was nonexistent in their lives while manic, or when I tried to commit suicide. Even with the lack of relationship my mother and I have, I still knew she was in mental torment. This disease is not picky; it latches on to even the best of us. Now I was suffering the embarrassment from being in a small community where I was well known due to my businesses. It was overwhelming.

When you're manic, your mind will only allow you to think of one thing: *How can I escape this madness? How can I get out of this horrible craziness in my mind?* After mania finally passes, it leaves you in the midst of disgust.

This time, I was not going to let all of these emotions get the best of me. I took my medications, and saw my therapist, and worked through all the guilt, shame, and remorse. Therapists are a wonderful tool to have in your corner, so that you have someone to run by all your crazy thoughts, feelings, and emotions—without judgment. You can check in with them, and they'll honestly let you know whether the thoughts and feelings you have are real or not real (bipolar); which ones matter, and which ones you ought to let go.

It was not easy working through all the guilt, shame, and remorse. After almost eight years, acceptance of myself and of my disease is still difficult. I know that having this disease for the rest of my life will always be hard to accept. As I do the next right thing with the aid of medications, I am relieved to know that I can maintain stability. With this disease, I have no choice but to plunge forward, and take what may come, good or bad.

My daughters are the love of my life, and today I can finally be the good mother again that I have longed to be. My bipolar is in no way perfect. Even while stable, I can still become defensive and hostile. I would never harm them. If things ever get dicey, they always know they have the option to leave and go stay with their father. I always tell them that they should be able to feel safe no matter where they are. They usually choose me, and then I battle with all my might whatever thoughts of hostility, or other bipolar tendencies I may be having. I only want to have peace and a wonderful evening with them.

For so many years, I was the perfect parent, a good mom who took them to daycare, helped out at their school, picked them up, and tucked them in at night. I know that my disease caused devastation—in their lives and in mine—but I cannot continue to blame myself no matter how much my heart hurts. I am aware that they have forgiven me. Now I know it is time for me to forgive myself. I am not at this stage yet, however; it is going to take me more time. Self-forgiveness will come; just not today. Still, I can see that it's possible in the future.

Chapter Fourteen

Finding Spirituality

Finding spirituality was a key step for me. I realized that God made us all unique. Some people are afflicted with health issues in other ways—mentally or physically, or they may have addiction issues. I will not minimize bipolar disease. It takes thousands and thousands of lives every year. It almost took mine. Certainly, if I had been placed in the mental institution, it would have devastated my life so severely, I don't know that I would have been able to overcome. Believing in God may not take my disease away, but faith is meant to help me through the trials of everyday life.

At Celebrate Recovery, I was told of a wonderful loving God Who erases our past when we ask, and Who will be there with us always, if we seek Him. This was an amazing fact for me. Celebrate Recovery did not judge me or my past, even though I haven't been able to completely let go of the grief. I know stormy days will always come and go; so it helps me to know there are people who care, who don't judge me or my disease. It is rare to find this acceptance.

This experience with Celebrate Recovery has made me a believer. I know there is a God watching over me. I had been ostracized and rejected before, but here I felt safe for the first time, and able to open my heart. I started to feel free. I learned who the real Darcie is. I was not that person full of madness. Our heart and soul make us who we are.

With the help of Celebrate Recovery, my inner self became filled with strength, joy, peace, and love. I knew I would still struggle with bipolar, but I also knew that on days of stability, I would not have to be that bipolar Darcie. Life goes on.

What would come next in my life would test my faith to the extreme. My mental health was about to be drastically tested. I would have to learn to hold on tight to the glimmer of hope which still burned within my newfound self.

Chapter Fifteen

More Astonishing News

One afternoon out of the blue, my mother called to say she had a routine doctor's appointment, and she wondered if I'd go with her. Not knowing the true reason for her appointment, I agreed to go. I was soon bewildered at what the doctor had to tell her. She had seen him previously, and had not made anyone aware of it. She was actually back in to get the results of a biopsy for a softball-sized tumor in her breast. I was shocked that she had not told me. The doctor came in and told us that the biopsy showed that she had very aggressive breast cancer. She would most definitely need chemotherapy and radiation.

It had now been a year and a half after my father passed. I believe my mother had known of the cancer in her breast for a very long time.

She allowed the surgeon to remove the very large mass that took half of her breast, he put radiation clips in place so she could start radiation soon after. Soon after that, she declined all treatment. She was going to face the inevitable on her own terms. She believed that God was going to heal her. She never explained to me why she had declined treatment, until later when she told me of her faith in God and said that He would indeed heal her. All things are possible with God, but it is also said that God helps those who help themselves. In addition to her beliefs about faith, I do believe that what she saw my father go through had an effect on her own decline. I did have my suspicions that watching what my father went through had scared her very much, and she did not want to face it.

I was so frightened. Fear did not consume me, however. If I had let that happen, it would have proved a great detriment to my sanity. I kept taking my medication, seeing my psychiatric nurse practitioner, and going to my therapist. I knew facing the death of my mother was going to test my mental stability immensely, but I was not going to allow madness, craziness, depression, or anything else take over my life.

Telling my two daughters about their grandma was extremely difficult. I had to remain very strong and give them hope. They had actually become very close to their grandmother, despite my relationship with her, and they loved her very much.

ॐ

Prior to my mother receiving this news, she had been traveling with her best friend, Teri. Teri had worked in the airline industry for years. She and my mother were great friends. They enjoyed a lot of the same interests. She and my mother had been traveling all over together for some time. After my mother's diagnosis, they continued to travel. Even when the cancer was spreading rapidly, my mother still went on these trips. It was so difficult for me, knowing she must have been in pain and wasn't saying a word to anyone. She had stopped talking to me about it entirely. She would talk to my brothers, convincing them not to worry, and to have the same faith that God was going to heal her. She would not allow any of us to ask about her pain or to talk about the cancer in any way. She had made her decision, and what I had to say was of no value to her.

As she traveled and denied treatment, I couldn't even keep up with all the places they would go together. I know they went to Belize,

Alaska, New York City, and more. While my mother was traveling, I tried to live my life as normal. It was extremely difficult.

I had applied for disability that year, and received it fairly quickly. While waiting for the disability money to come through I was searching for odd jobs here and there to stay afloat. I had lost my car in the bankruptcy, so I learned to walk a lot each day. This was partially how I had lost the weight from Harvard. I became obsessed with walking. Even when I was offered a ride from friends, I would turn them down. I received a lot of peace and solitude and some of my best thinking while walking.

CR

It had now been a year since my mother was diagnosed. I contacted the doctor without her knowing, to see how much it had spread. I was concerned and scared. I did not have anyone to talk to. She had forbidden me to speak to the doctor, but that did not stop me. I knew he would have some sort of information, as she was still going to see him. I had no idea why she was doing that. She would visit the doctor, but then not do anything he suggested.

I believe Mom finally resigned herself to the realization that maybe God was not choosing to heal her. The doctor explained to me that it had spread to her bones, and that she had a tumor in one of her lungs. I will never know where her strength was coming from. When she found out that I knew about the metastasis, she was furious that I had called the doctor.

A little while later, my mother's cousin passed away. We were at the funeral, and while there, for the first time I saw my mother as weak and tired. I knew I really needed someone to talk to. My mother never knew how hard it was for me to keep her secret from everyone. I could not speak to my brothers about it. They would only accuse me of having no faith that she would be healed. She had brainwashed them. My Aunt Jan, with whom my mother was extremely close, was there at the funeral. I went over to talk to her, and decided I could not hold it in any longer. I told Jan of my mother's cancer. She was shocked to hear of this, since they had always been so close. (I called her my aunt, but she was really my cousin.) Jan was slightly younger than my mother, and I knew she was the best person for me to talk to. My mother went over and sat down beside her to chitchat. My Aunt Jan asked my mother how she was feeling. My mother was instantly furious. She asked, "Darcie told you, didn't she?"

Jan told her, "It's not Darcie's fault. She is just concerned, and needed to tell someone."

After that, my mother named my oldest brother as her healthcare representative. She was using her normal coping skill of denial, and believed that even without treatment God would heal her. Two months later, my brother took her to the emergency room. They did a brain scan, and found that she had three brain tumors. I was not prepared for this news. We were told that she had approximately three months to live.

All this strain was taking a huge toll on me emotionally. I was so afraid that I would break, and mania or depression would creep in. However, I continued to take my medication and see my therapist and doctor, in order to retain the brain capacity to be there for my mother.

That weekend, my mother was in excruciating pain. I went to be with her. No matter what drugs from the emergency room they gave her, none of them would take away the pain, or even ease it. I called her doctor and explained that she needed something stronger. He eventually prescribed something that finally helped.

While I was on the phone with the doctor, my oldest brother, the so-called healthcare representative, came in and started screaming at me. He asked first who I was talking with, and when I told him I was talking to the doctor, he became furious, telling me, "I am supposed to be the one to take care of this! Get off the phone!"

I told him no. He was drunk. He came up about three inches from my face, and said, "I am going to smash your mouth in!"

I said, "Go ahead."

He came up behind me and said he was going to smash my head in, and again I told him to go ahead.

My mother was in so much pain while he was acting this way. Her head was hanging way low, as she had a large tumor on the back of her neck, and the pain was excruciating. She was hearing what he was saying and she eventually gained enough strength to yell at him to "get the hell out." He left, broke a bunch of beer bottles outside, and sped off. I called the police, but they never found him. I just wanted them to evaluate him mentally.

I was able to get Mom's pain somewhat under control after talking with the doctor, at least for that evening. It started over again the next day, so I just repeated the medications he had given to me for her. My heart was breaking, she was in so much pain. She would go outside for a few minutes, and then want to come back in. There were several steps down to the outside patio, and it was very hard for me to help move her from step to step. My mother was not a large woman by any means; but helping her was one thing, and lifting her was a different story. The stress was taking its toll on me, and I knew I could not possibly do this anymore by myself.

I told my mother that I really needed someone to help me. I think she knew that I was right. I knew that a nurse or another stranger would be out of the question. I asked her about my Aunt Jan, and she said yes. So I called Jan, and she came that night. Mom was scheduled to see the doctor the next day. Per her request, the doctor referred her to a radiologist, for radiation treatment for the brain. My mother had already figured out that radiation would shrink the brain tumors and lessen the pain. She decided that she would rather pass away from the lungs filling up with fluid rather than from brain cancer.

The doctor agreed with that decision. They started radiation immediately, and within one week she was feeling much better. She continued the radiation for two months. It seemed that my mother had her own plan all along.

☞

Since my mother started feeling much better with the radiation treatments, she and my aunt started acting like kids again. It was good to see my mother laughing and carrying on. We knew she had only approximately two and a half months left, but she was going to enjoy them.

With my aunt there to help, and my mother doing as well as could be expected, I thankfully started spending some nights at home again with my girls. This also allowed me to get my rest, and to go to Celebrate

Recovery, and back to my psychiatric nurse practitioner and therapist. I was doing very well, considering what was happening, and I knew I had to stay this way. *Stability is the key to living life with bipolar.* Whatever comes our way, we have to take charge and trust that with a spiritual connection, continuing medication, doctors, and therapists, we can maintain stability in our lives. We don't have to become manic or depressed. We will have ups and downs during periods of stability—mostly mild—as I experience. They are not anything anyone can talk me out of or that I can talk myself down from. Stability is a choice.

Cℜ

One of the highlights for me in my mother's last few months was that for the first time ever, my mother went with me to one of my psychiatrist's appointments. I had to have another opinion from a psychiatrist, for my disability benefits. Just having her there to validate my illness was amazing. She had always been there for my brother with schizophrenia, but had never acknowledged that maybe I needed help and attention, too.

Cℜ

My mother was getting weaker and weaker now. They had to stop the radiation treatments. Hospice care said that she had about two weeks left. The hospice social worker started talking with me by phone, or she would make a visit out to check in with the family. I think she sensed my mother's household was pretty dysfunctional. My two oldest brothers were nowhere to be found during those last couple of weeks. In her last few days, I kept wondering, *How can this be happening? She is so young.*

Mom was 61. I was 37 now, and I was not ready to lose my mother. It was hard for me to talk to my daughters. They were going to miss her so much.

The night before she died, I knelt down on the floor next to her bed. She was in so much pain and agony. I asked her if she wanted me to anoint her with oil, like it says in the Bible about healing, and she said yes. Her faith was not wavering. I had never anointed anyone before, so I had to ask her where the oil was, and which scriptures to read. So I placed a drop of oil on her now bald head, and read the Scriptures, and added a few prayers of my own. Although my mother was clearly passing, I knew that anointing her would bring her some peace. I wanted to acknowledge this for her, and let her know that I too have a great deal of faith, even though I also believe in modern medicine.

The next day, my mother's breathing was getting louder and louder, with her time of death approaching very soon. I lay next to her on her bed a lot that day. I had to leave at times, when it felt too unbearable. She was not responding anymore. Her body was going through the final process of dying. We tried to keep her comfortable but it was very hard. She continued to be in a lot of pain. Hearing her cry out in pain was so horrible for me. I sobbed and sobbed. I kept praying for God to let her go and finally be out of pain.

My grandmother was there now. It was my Aunt Jan, my grandmother, and myself.

I left my mother's room just for a moment. As I stepped back into the hallway I did not hear any noise, so I ran back in. She had passed away. I cried out to my aunt and grandma. I had never heard my grandmother cry. It was agonizing. My heart was breaking for her, and for losing her daughter.

My brothers never showed up that night. I called hospice care, and they came out to get information for the death certificate and to remove some medical devices. My aunt and I dressed my mother and called the funeral home.

My mother looked so peaceful and beautiful. Unlike my father when he died, her face was full of grace, faith, and hope. This was a relief for me. But nothing would take away my anguish, nor comfort my insurmountably hurting heart.

☙

When I saw the grace and beauty upon my mother's face when she passed, it reassured me our Heavenly Father had been waiting for my beautiful, faithful mother. It is so hard to see your mother, whom you have truly always loved, not wish you all the best in life. She had never apologized to me for the past. Still, thankfully, the peace of heaven had happened for her. It was done.

My mother passed on November 10, 2007. Three years and one day after my father. I started planning her funeral right away. My brothers still did not step in and help, or even give any input. They did not see her during the last five days of her life. I believe that the anguish would have been too much for them, so avoidance was better for them; or maybe I'm simply making excuses for them. At any rate, it was not pleasant to see the way they had acted. The funeral went very well, but it was definitely a relief when it was over.

My Aunt Jan later told me that my mother had admitted to her in her last two months that over the last few years she had harbored a lot of animosity towards me, which she's really felt about me since I was a child. My mother's hostility is very hard for me to understand. My aunt believed that my mother had been very jealous of my success over the years. My mother's life is over. Now I will move on into the future, which will no longer involve her.

ೞ

Suddenly, extreme overwhelming sadness crept up on me. I called my friend Samantha, and told her I wanted to go to the beach. I wanted to get drunk. I had not had any alcohol in two months. She came, and we drove to the beach. I still had a little cabin there, which had not been taken back yet. We started drinking as soon as we arrived at the cabin before heading to the bar. By the time we arrived at the bar we were already drunk. We went up to the bar, ordered a drink, and then both of us headed to the bathroom. We started vomiting right away. We came out, and the bartender said she had already called us a cab. Well, that night did not turn out as I had expected. It was a humiliating experience. Only I knew what was going on in my life, which made the acceptance of humiliation easier.

It was time to face life again. I went to my psychiatric nurse practitioner to check in, and I also went to see my therapist. I continued in Celebrate Recovery. I was able to stay stable once again—by the grace of God and with sheer determination that bipolar was not going to get the best of me—even at this horrible time in my life.

Chapter Sixteen

When the Rain Comes Down

Immediately after my mother's death, following my mother's wishes, I had become the official caregiver for my grandmother. We had to revise her will and power of attorney. I was solely responsible for my grandmother now. This was hard for me. Not that I did not want to take care of her; I loved her with all my heart and soul. It was hard because it brought up feelings about my mother. I felt that my mom should have been there to take care of her, because after all she was her daughter. I was just the granddaughter. As much as my mother would have liked to have been there, it was not going to happen. My grandmother was 85, and still going strong.

❧

It had been five months now since my mother's death, and now my grandmother was losing her husband. He had kidney cancer and COPD. They had been married for 25 years. He passed away just six months after my mother. He had family from his first marriage, and thankfully they planned the funeral. I was fairly close to him, but he had entered my life when I was ten or so. My grandmother and I had a very strong bond. I had not cared for him at first, because he was interrupting my relationship with her. He was certainly what my grandmother needed in her life, however.

After my grandfather's death, my grandmother became very lonely. She had never been much of a television watcher, partly because she could not see very well. I would visit her as much as I could. My daughters were only seven and eleven, and I was coaching my youngest daughter's basketball team, doing my best to make up for the past. All of the death had taken me away from them a lot, just as the manic times had done. I was feeling wonderful again, as I had reasoned with Mom's death and was moving on.

Nevertheless, guilt about Grandma being alone would tear me up inside. I knew she needed me, but my children needed me too. So many times, I was at a loss as to what to do. When I would visit her, she would be sitting in her chair and listening to the television. I would ask her what was playing on TV, and she would say, "Oh, nothing." She was so funny. I knew she turned it on just for the noise. People's voices, places, and all the motions of life were inside that box for her. Thankfully, when my mother was alive, she used to bring over large-print copies of *Readers' Digest*. Grandma would read the same ones over and over.

Grandma did have some health issues. She had dementia, congestive heart failure, and diabetes. I was very fortunate to have a caregiver on the property, my step-grandfather's daughter-in-law. She worked for about four hours a day. She would make sure Grandma took her pills and got her insulin shot, and she also helped with meals. That was all my grandma needed at the time.

CR

Grandma was doing okay, and things were relatively calm for about six months; but then my grandmother received a phone call at 1:00 a.m.: news that my uncle with schizophrenia was in the hospital.

He was dying of pneumonia and COPD. When we arrived, he was already in the process of death, which by now was all too familiar to me. My grandmother went up to him and told him how much she loved him. My aunt had come, too. My grandmother wanted to go home and get some clothes, so she could spend the night. We thought we had plenty of time. By the time we arrived back at the hospital, he had just passed, less than five minutes before. Again, I had to hear cries of agony, this time from my grandmother. She was a very strong woman, but she had just lost her daughter, husband, and son in the space of only 18 months. I had to plan the funeral for my uncle. My grandmother did not have any money. She actually used her Social Security check to pay the expenses.

By now I really had to wonder what the reason was behind all of this suffering and pain. Seeing my grandmother in this state was more than I could bear. I poured my heart out to God. *Please, God, help me make it through this without jeopardizing my mental health.* I had to be able to take care of Grandma. She was my angel in disguise. I would go to the ends of the earth for her. I could not let my grandma down. I was the last one left, designated to take care of her. But she still had her sister, with whom she had a wonderful kinship, and she was also close to my Aunt Jan.

ભ

As it turned out, my uncle's funeral was very nice. We did not expect anyone to show up, but a nice surprise happened: People showed up from a mental illness association in town called Options. These folks had helped him a lot through the years; they would get him one-hour jobs here and there, and helped him to feel useful.

Twenty people showed up, which just proved to me that he was the most gentle man you would ever want to meet. He had never hurt anyone. They shared many stories about him. My grandma may not have laughed, but she was thankful for them coming to honor him. As a surprise, they brought with them a check for Grandma. It was a true blessing. She would not have had enough money to live on that month if that check had not been given to her. It was enough money to cover all of the funeral expenses. My sweet grandma looked at that check, and said, "What do we do with it?"

I laughed, and told her, "We will put it in the bank. It was money that belonged to your son."

After my uncle died, Grandma started doing poorly. Mainly, her mind was deteriorating. She worried excessively about anything and everything. With her husband, daughter, and son gone, a lot of anxiety built up in her. She worried about me and all her grandkids— meaning my brothers, who did *not* show up constantly to see her. She was alone, which didn't help. I kept feeling that I was not there enough for her. I piled up a lot of guilt onto myself. Yet, a part of me just wanted to be free from any people needing me. The caregiver still came in, three to four hours a day; but it just was not enough for Grandma.

 beginning ornament

Due to all the stress, sorrow, and anxiety, Grandma came down with shingles. She had them on her face and head. It was so painful for her. I spoke to her on the phone, and I spoke to the caregiver, but I could not bring myself to go see her. Her face was covered with the shingles, and I could not bear to see her like that. I realize it was a cop-out on my part, but I decided I would make up for it later on.

Her shingles never went away completely. One eye was still having breakouts. She was in extreme pain much of the time. My grandmother was against pain medication other than aspirin, but once she contracted the shingles, she was taking pain medication every four hours.

She was trying to survive all the devastation in her life. She was never the same after the shingles. Shingles had actually caused her to have several mini-strokes. She started getting up in the middle of the night, and going to the front door to get out. Thankfully, she could not get the door open. She had fallen out of bed twice due to low blood sugar, and went to the emergency room three times in three weeks. Every time she would fall, unconscious like that, and I would be in the emergency room with her, she remained unresponsive. I would think, *This is it. She is going to die.* But then hours later, she would wake up. They called it a diabetic coma.

Life had become all about death for me. I know the things I was doing to take care of myself were saving me from myself. Still, so many times I asked myself, *Is this life worth it?* In my thought, the only answer I would hear back was, *Set an example through your losses and agony.*

My grandmother's sister and my Aunt Jan insisted that Grandma should stay in her home, but the doctors were telling me that she was not safe, that she would need 24-hour care. They said she needed to be in a nursing home. This became the most difficult decision I had to make. I knew I really didn't have any other choice, because I wanted her to be safe. With her dementia and diabetes combined, we simply could not manage. When I finally placed her in a nursing home, I knew it was the best decision.

I was afraid she might get worse, but instead she started thriving. She had people to interact with, and the nurses and staff absolutely loved her. I was so thankful that she never asked me questions about why I put her in the nursing home. Sometimes, she would say she wanted to go home, and that saddened me. But overall, her health was relatively good.

As the dementia became worse, she began not to recognize several of her relatives. This was expected, so we just moved along at her pace. Her sister and niece would go visit her almost every day, and sometimes take her out for the afternoon. She enjoyed that. I was thankful. Everyone deserves a grandmother like her. She was so loved by anyone she ever met, and everyone would comment on her sweetness.

Chapter Seventeen

Challenges of Faith

In 2008, I was doing everything well to maintain mental stability, including seeing my therapist and psychiatric nurse practitioner. I was also taking care of my physical health, too. I was exercising at least five days a week, and watching what I was eating. I had gained a lot of weight while I was at Harvard, during all the medication trials.

I decided to go to a urologist, because I had been having some issues with my bladder. The doctor opted for a sling to hold my bladder up to avoid further issues. He said my bladder had weakened due to giving birth to large babies. My youngest was born at ten pounds, one ounce. She was fifteen now and playing basketball. My oldest was in her second year of college and 5'3". She followed the genes on her father's side. She had the height and beauty of her grandmother and great aunt.

My bladder surgery went well. The next step was to go in for a women's exam. I had not had one in years. I asked my doctor if I should have a mammogram due to my family history. She agreed that it certainly wouldn't hurt. After the mammogram, they decided to do an ultrasound. The technician kept going over this one spot. I could tell there was something there. When she finished, she told me she was going to get the radiologist to read the results quickly. Then the radiologist came in, and said that I had an abnormal-looking lump in my left breast. She scheduled me for a biopsy, and referred me to a surgeon as well.

I waited six weeks for those results. They said they had to send the sample to San Francisco, California, because they were not able to get a clear decision from our labs here in Oregon. After the six weeks, I went to the surgeon, and he told me the lump should be removed. He said it had some black spots in it but it was not cancerous. It was called ductile hyperplasia. My mother had suffered from ductile carcinoma.

I had the lump removed, and the doctor said everything was fine, and to have another mammogram in six to nine months. During this time, I never said one word about the bladder surgery or the breast lump removal to my grandmother. She would have worried herself sick, and there was not anything to worry about, anyway. It was all taken care of.

CR

Thirteen months later, I went in for my second mammogram. This time, the girl doing the ultrasound did not say anything during the exam. I received a phone call two days later from my primary care doctor saying that I needed to make an appointment.

I made the appointment and went in to see her. Now I was in her office in my gown, and I sat there praying, knowing a Power above me was there with me. Not yet knowing the results of my test, I anxiously awaited. I was shocked by what she had to say about the mammogram. She explained that I now had two more lumps in my left breast, two new ones in my right breast, and twelve lesions.

I was 39 at the time. I asked her what she would do in my situation. She simply asked, "How far are you willing to go to save your life?"

That made it very clear to me that I was going to need to have a double mastectomy. I was not really afraid. I looked at it this way: If my mother would have taken care of the breast cancer before her lump became the size of a softball, she would still be alive today.

Even though I was not really afraid of the surgery, I longed for my mother—for her reassurance, her touch—just to see her face. This surgery was going to be the hardest surgery I had ever gone through in my life. I was extremely thankful for my loving friends, but nothing can replace a mother being beside you, and being there when you awake. I knew of course this could not be the case, and harsh reality set in again. I knew my bipolar was going to be tested. All the harsh drugs mixed with Lithium, Lamictal, Clonazepam, and Seroquel, I feared not only for my wellness but also for my sanity.

I did not realize the extent of the pain my daughters were going through over my impending surgery. They would not open up to me right away. Their hearts were pouring out love for me, wondering, *Is mommy going to die of breast cancer like Grandma did?*

The image of their little faces when I came out of surgery will stay with me forever. I knew they were scared, but children show love and pain in so many different ways. I assured them everything was going to be just fine, and that I was taking care of the problem before it became cancer.

The doctors believed that the lumps and lesions were still in the pre-cancer hyperplasia stage; they wouldn't know for sure until after the surgery. I had the surgery done in 2009. While in surgery, there was a plastic surgeon there as well. The plastic surgeon did the reconstruction, which I also wanted. So the surgeon removed the breasts and some lymph nodes. Tested, the lymph nodes came back pre-cancerous. Then the plastic surgeon placed a bag, a port, and a drain, and sewed me back up. As instructed, I never stopped taking my bipolar medications.

I arrived back home after one day in the hospital, and was coming off the drugs they had given me with the IV. I started to have some pain, so I took the pain pills they gave me, along with all of my bipolar medications. My body did not react well. It was only the second day out of surgery, and I became irritable, agitated, and extremely anxious. I explained to the person who was there taking care of me that I had to leave. She did not know what to do. I walked out the front door with the drains hanging from my sides and completely out of my mind.

I walked around my subdivision, and when I finally arrived back home, a car belonging to a wonderful friend of mine was in my driveway. My friend taking care of me did not know what to do, so she called another friend of mine, and asked her to come by and offer some assistance in getting me into a better frame of mind. So I went in the car with my friend, and she asked me where I would like to go. I responded, "Turtle Lane."

Turtle Lane was one of my favorite serene places on the river. I had forgotten that we had to walk over several rocks to get down there, but I made it, and we sat down. We talked, but not about my situation. Her grandmother was starting to go through some of the same health issues that my grandmother had started in on about two years before. So we talked a lot about her grandmother, and what my friend was going to have to do. I wanted to keep my mind off of myself, so this helped immensely. I had no desire to talk about my surgery. The sight of my breast being cut off had sickened me now.

I stayed as well as I could regarding the outcome, and that is how I was able to get through the next six months of reconstruction. After my friend and I talked on the river bank for a little while, I had started feeling some pain. I told her I should get home. In the state of madness I had been in when I left the house, I had not felt any pain. It is amazing how our minds can change our perception of fear. It reminds me of going to the dentist: When I am getting the shot of Novocaine, I keep reminding myself to think of something else—a good experience, a relaxing waterfall, or the beach—whatever works for me at that time. On this day, a good friend, a good talk, and the serenity of Turtle Lane and the river brought me through, and restored my sanity.

After four weeks, I was to go in for my first saline injection. The doctor started off with 50 cc in each breast. He had taken the drains out and administered the saline into the ports on my side. Each week, I went in for another injection. Each time it stretched the skin further and further, and it became more painful. I started taking pain pills on the way there and on the way back. I would be in pain for a couple of days after each time; until near the end, when the pain finally became so intolerable that I told him, "No more injections. I am done." I did not reach the size I had set out to have, but I was still comfortable with my decision. So I went in for my next surgery, which was approximately six months later to have the bags removed and the implants placed.

CR

Years have passed now, and I am happy with the decision I made. I have never had anyone say anything negative about my breasts. I am not ashamed of them. As with bipolar, sometimes we do not have a choice about what we have to go through. But we can choose to accept who we are. Each day with bipolar can be a struggle. We wish we could get up at the crack of dawn and go to work like other people, we wish our moods wouldn't fluctuate up and down all day. And always, God forbid mania or depression—because either one can creep in and suddenly erupt, like a massive explosion. I do know that no matter what, God is always with me, but He will allow the life I have been given to proceed.

When my mastectomy and reconstruction had been finished for about eight months, I was having some good times with my children and my grandmother. After about six more months, I decided I should go in for another women's exam. I had been experiencing some horrible pain each month. It was 2010 now. When I went in, I met with the gynecologist, and she wanted to do an ultrasound. They found a tumor in my right ovary, as well as fibroids, which they thought was the cause of the pain. They wanted to do a hysterectomy. It was to be done laparoscopically: just remove the tumor, the cervix, and the fibroids. I was not going to be having any more children, and I wanted to be out of pain. They scheduled my surgery right away.

Grandma was still in the nursing home and doing pretty well. She was 88 now. She had some setbacks once in a while that were a little worrisome to me; but I knew I had to focus on my own health. When she had her setbacks, they would put her on complete bed rest, which was not a good idea, because my grandmother had the will of a tiger going after its prey. She would not stay in that bed. So then they put an alarm on her bed. She would get up, and it would sound, and then she would say, "What the devil is that thing going off for?" She was so feisty, even at 88 years old. Her face was priceless.

What was at the outset supposed to be a relatively easy surgery, taking 90 minutes, instead took over three and a half hours, and I lost three and a half pints of blood. The doctor and her staff decided to remove the uterus first, but it was frozen and would not move. The uterus, ovaries, and bowels were scarred, thick with lesions. Due to the findings, the doctor decided to open me up, as she thought it was endometriosis. After the surgery, the results came back that I had pre-cancerous cells on my cervix, and the ovary that was suspicious was also pre-cancerous.

I came out of that surgery and was stunned at what had happened. Instead of having a fairly easy procedure, I would now have to be down for several weeks. The only thing that saved me from a bipolar reaction was that I could not get up without a little help.

They had to adjust my pain medication several times to find the one that mixed well with my bipolar medications. I was not about to stop my bipolar medications. I would rather endure the pain than experience the madness of the bipolar, which would also mean I wouldn't be able to be there for my grandmother and my children.

During this time, my grandmother started asking a lot of questions about me. It had been two weeks since I had seen her. I broke down and called her to let her know I was okay. I told her about the surgery, and she seemed to be okay with it. I was thankful that my Aunt Jan and my grandmother's sister had been visiting her almost every day. I went to see her myself after that. I was still in pain, but I needed to see her to let her know that I really was alright.

Thinking about the surgeries tempted me to go back to my old ways. I will not deny that. That is the bipolar in me. I was bitter. It feared that some cancer was going to take me, sooner or later. These health issues were seemingly insurmountable to me. Then, I reminded myself that I have been given gifts along this journey of bipolar. I am a mess at times, full of rage and irritability. This only lasts for a day; but I will never give up this fight. I also know that with bipolar, thoughts of suicide may come randomly or frequently.

I tell you, if you are doing illegal drugs and taking bipolar medications, you may as well throw the bipolar medications out the window, because they will do nothing for you. Taking illegal drugs will not make you well. Illegal drugs will only kill you. Your madness will become completely out of control, and you will keep wanting more drugs. Soon you will die, leaving behind your wonderful family. If you have children, would you want to leave them behind? *Is it worth it*? *No*! Ask God for help when the despair or madness comes. He can stabilize you. If you haven't been taking medications, then He will show you where to turn. I promise: It will not be to prescription or street drugs.

The proper unique bipolar medications for you will work wonders. *We have bipolar, but we can be strong. There is great power that comes from asking God for help.* I would not exist today without my faith, my determination, and my knowledge that the only way we will survive is to take the medications. Even though it may make us feel numb sometimes, it never will be worth it to stop taking them.

Chapter Eighteen

Glimpses of Freedom

After everything was completed with my hysterectomy, I was able to start spending more time with Grandma. I felt some freedom again. No longer did I feel like there was a cloud over my head everywhere I walked. We had a nice summer in 2010. I am a fan of anything that has to do with the outdoors. That summer, I was kayaking, swimming, hiking, or going to the beach as much as possible. I would go with some of my close friends. Whenever I get myself to the beach or at a river, it is like I am a kid again; but now, even more, I had a great feeling of freedom. I love running on the beach, playing football, or building bonfires. With as much time as I spent all those years as a kid at my parents' property on the beach, we never did these things; we just weren't allowed to.

Enjoying the beauty of the outdoors in general brings me down to earth and back to my true inner self. I also realize at the same time what a majestic God we have, and how He gave us all this for our pleasure. I love to just gaze upon His beautiful creation. When we contemplate the beauty of the ocean, or magnificent waterfalls, how can we deny that there is a God? Obviously, The One Who cares so much about us gave all of this to us to enjoy.

When winter came, we had some snow that year. I love the snow: I love to watch it fall and hit my nose. My favorite memories are watching my children when they were small play in the snow. When I was at McLean in Boston, in one night 17 inches of snow fell. I guess they were no strangers to this type of storm, but I was in complete amazement. I did not have a desire to play in it, because it was also about ten degrees below zero. It stayed frozen. I wondered how people made it into work, but everyone just took it in stride. In the building I was staying in at the time, along the sidewalks there were giant icicles hanging, which looked like daggers to me. I was told that people had been killed by them. I had been so ignorant about what the weather was going to be like, so I came completely unprepared. I remember I had to have someone drive me to town to get a new coat, scarf, and hat. In Oregon, we maybe get four to six inches at the very most, and then it is forty degrees during the day. People from all over the Valley actually call in sick to work when that happens. It is fascinating to me how different it can be in other parts of the world.

Chapter Nineteen

Losing My Sweetness

My grandmother's health was now taking a turn for the worse. She was 89 years of age. I knew she would not live forever, but I was never going to be prepared to lose her. She was my biggest fan, even through all of her years she lived in poverty. My grandmother had to work her fingers to the bone trying to support her family. She did picking in the bulb fields and hop fields, or she picked mint, and sometimes cotton. I believe the hard work is what made her so strong. The poverty was passed on to my grandmother from her mother and father. My grandmother was the oldest of four children. She and her sister were the only ones left now.

I was glad that I had been able to build a new house for my grandmother when she and my step-grandfather were in their mid-eighties. At the time, the house they'd been living in was not on a foundation, and all of the doorways were way too small for a handicapped person. When it would come time for a walker or a wheelchair, they would have had to go into a nursing home simply due to their poor living conditions. They did not quite understand this then, but I knew that if they wanted to live on their property, the old house had to go. It was rat-infested and the floors were slanted, so I had been truly afraid for their safety. I had been able to get a reverse mortgage, as I knew that they would not have been able to afford a monthly payment. I also wanted my grandmother for once in her life to have a beautiful home to live in. I was glad that I had at least been able to do that for Grandma. She had been able to stay in that new home for a few good years, before I had to put her in the nursing home.

But now I was starting to lose her. Grandma's dementia and congestive heart failure were getting worse. She was still mobile for seven days before she had to go on her last bed rest. I was lucky to have one more glimpse of my grandma's humor during that last week. I had come to visit, and I asked her if she would like to take a ride in the wheelchair to get a cup of coffee, and she said yes. At the cafeteria, we sat down at a table and an older man came and sat across from us. My grandmother looked at him, and asked, "How old are you?"

He replied, "I am 85."

She said, "Well, you're getting up there, aren't you?"

He was a little upset, but I couldn't help but laugh. She was so innocent. She had no idea that she had just insulted him. Kind of like when she would go to a yard sale, and ask if they would take a nickel for a set of dishes.

My smile quickly faded. I thought, *I can't believe she is leaving me.*

We went back to her room, and, as it turns out, she never left her room again. Her lungs were pooling with fluid, causing her heart to fail. I stayed overnight in the nursing home every night. I was not going to leave her side. I wanted her to know I was there the entire time with her. I was desperate at this point.

Staff members at this nursing home did not deal well with patients who were passing. They provided only minimal care. We had been given some poor nursing staff, and Grandma was in a lot of pain. We were at a loss. My Aunt Jan found out that we could bring a hospice worker in to provide direct care. When I talked to hospice care on the phone, they said they would take over, they would communicate right away with the director of the home, and they would give Grandma everything she needed. I knew God was there to help us to let Grandma go gently. Hospice care made sure that when we knew she was in pain, they would give her more pain medicine. The nursing staff had tried to stop giving me food while I stayed with her; but hospice care made sure I received the food I needed. We also were given a private room with two extra beds. Hospice has saved my sanity so many times. With their love and support, hospice has given what was needed, every time I have lost a family member.

We were finally able to get her pain under control. My cousin and I stayed with Grandma every night until she was gone. My grandmother may have been living in a nursing home, but we made sure that she passed with the dignity and respect she deserved. God had given her a good long life. I have never met anyone who had overcome so much adversity in her lifetime.

I have sometimes wondered over the years: *God, how much more do I have to endure before I break?* I thought losing my sweet Grandma would do it for me, but again I asked for His strength and courage to carry through, and I asked for my sanity to stay intact. I continued taking my medications, exercising, and seeing my therapist. And my sanity did indeed stay intact, due to my knowledge and diligence, by the grace of God.

Chapter Twenty

Grandmother's Funeral

My grandmother's funeral was the hardest for me to plan. Grandma passed away on April 2, 2011. In my grandmother's case, age did not matter to me. She was who she was at 60 or at 100. I would miss her like no one else. Her spirit never wavered. With her positive outlook on life, she showed me that even with poverty and trials, it is a beautiful spirit and true inner self that make it possible for us to overcome many obstacles. My grandmother was the truest woman ever in my life, transparent to the world. She was always worried about other people. I don't believe she once felt sorry for herself.

While staying at the nursing home, she had asked frequently where my brothers were, and why they wouldn't come to see her. They had kept themselves away from the sadness and despair. Eventually, she would not have recognized them anyway.

I planned the funeral for my grandma for the following weekend. Her funeral turned out to be beautiful. There were a lot of people there. I decided not to involve a pastor or chaplain. I felt compelled to do Grandma's eulogy myself. I believed that no one, other than her sister, knew Grandma better than I did. I wanted to tell the story of her life—the true grandma I had, not what a clergyman might say about her. Grandma was unique, special, and she had a heart of gold. She was unbelievable to me. I wanted everyone at that funeral to know where her sweet spirit now resided. It all went very well.

I have countless memories of Grandma. Every time I would go to her house, she would have something for me: a little stuffed animal or toy. I knew she probably picked it up at a yard sale. It did not matter to me. This reminds me of a book my mother had given to my oldest daughter when she was seven. It is called *Something to Remember Me By,* by Susan B. Vosack. In the story, every time a little girl goes to see her grandma, the grandma gives her a small token, or toy. The little girl would ask her grandma what it was for, and the grandmother would say, "It is something to remember me by." It is an amazing little book for all children and adults, about love and aging. Thinking of the things my grandma had done for me like this, it was easy for me to share about her sweet spirit and her unconditional love, and her unintentionally funny sense of humor and not-so-funny insults at times. I wanted to send her off to be with God, with everyone knowing what a wonderful woman and grandmother she had been. The song *Amazing Grace* was played at her funeral.

We also had a small graveside funeral, with just me, my Aunt Jan, and my two cousins. We entered her ashes into the ground, and began singing *Amazing Grace*. It was very hard to dig the hole and bury her ashes, but it was to honor my grandmother and how much I loved her. It was heart-wrenching and gratifying at the same time. I knew God was there that day to get me through something I had never dreamed of having to do. I was thankful to have three people by my side who have always been with me, especially the wonderful woman who made my mother's world so much brighter at the end of her life: my Aunt Jan.

Chapter Twenty-one

Blindsided

The day after my grandmother passed, I went to get my hair done for her funeral, which was coming up that weekend. As I started to go into the salon, I received a phone call that my oldest brother (who was 47) had passed away—the night before grandmother had passed. He had suffered a massive heart attack. I was shocked. I called his girlfriend, bawling, wanting to know what had happened. There were never any warning signs. Doctors said he had cardiomyopathy, which simply means heart failure.

He was the brother who had threatened me when my mother was dying. It did not matter now though; I still loved him very much. This world can be an ugly place, but we can make room for the good even when evil hearts can run rampant. You never know when you can be the one to change just one person's heart, even a little at a time. My brother and I had not spoken in many years. When we were young, I looked up to him. He was six years older, and he had nice cars. He was able to work, and he did not have to be at home. He was free to go wherever he wished. I didn't see him much after he turned 16. I missed him. During high school he met a girl and they were later married. My sister-in-law became pregnant, and they had a little girl. She is now in her twenties. Unfortunately, my brother and sister-in-law did not stay married long, divorcing when my niece was young.

My niece suffered a great loss, losing her father so young, but she stayed very strong, and planned a nice funeral for him. She spoke, and a chaplain spoke as well. I had not planned on speaking; however, because of the eulogy I had given at my grandmother's funeral, the funeral director asked me to speak. Even though my brother and I had been estranged for a few years, I did the best I could. I talked about how, deep down, he was a wonderful man, and I added a lot in there about forgiveness.

This next fact is so poignant, and truly a blessing to me. Even though my niece had no knowledge of which funeral home my grandmother (her great-grandmother) was in, she chose to send my brother's body to the same exact funeral home. To me, it felt like this was a rekindling of their spirits, making up for so much lost time. I saw it as God's way of having them ascend to heaven together. I can just imagine them holding hands and going off to paradise. Truly amazing.

Yes some truly remarkable things happened with each illness and sickness. During these periods of anguish and sadness, my bipolar did take a hold of me a day here and there, where I just could not take on any responsibility at all. I would even revert back to the old ways on occasion, and go have a couple of drinks. I always came back around fairly quickly. *I've never truly understood why having bipolar wasn't enough suffering. Why add, on top of all that, the cancer and the deaths? To test me?*

Chapter Twenty-two

Miss Them, But Let Them Go: Claiming Myself and Being One with God

I had to come to terms with so much death in my family. To this day, I can sit within what once was, and grieve. Words, laughter, and pain. Grandma's smile. My mother's laugh. My uncle's ramblings. It is okay. But sometimes I would rather not hear them at all. Everything I looked forward to, like wonderful Thanksgivings and other holidays, would be no more. I spend a lot of holidays mostly alone. My ex-husband still has his mother, father, and other relatives, so I let my children go with him. So whenever it's a holiday, they'll come to be with me in the morning for a couple hours, and then go with him to his family's place for the holidays. I don't want them to miss out on the meaning of the holidays, or to miss out on being with family just because my own family is gone. I know there are a lot of people who don't understand this reasoning, and ask why would I allow it to be this way on holidays. Truth is, some day my children will be grown, and they will have their own families, and I will have my grandchildren. Due to my unselfishness now, making peace after these horrible times of my life, they will remember what I did for them, and I know I will experience the best holidays yet.

Since writing out these feelings, I have learned that each of our loved ones has an impact in our lives in different ways. No death is the same, of course. Some family members I do miss more deeply than others, like my grandmother. She was very much the unselfish one, and she would've done the exact thing I'm doing about the holidays.

The deep feelings I have for my mother, father, and grandmother will always be the hardest to bear: devastating, overwhelming, and sad.

〇ℛ

You may be wondering, how did I stay sane through all this? I stayed sane through pure stubbornness. Stubbornness can go a long way. Yes, at times my sanity was tested. When the grief would come in, and along with it anger, madness, and moments of craziness, pushing me to the brink, darkness would shadow me, and sometimes take me momentarily back to old habits. But I had made the decision that I will always battle my demons. *God is bigger than those demons.*

I am no different from any other bipolar individual. My hope for all of us with bipolar is that in times of devastation, we will never give in. There is always a light out of the darkness. When I cycled back and forth, with each experience of adversity, *I always kept my eyes on God.* This focus gave me faith, hope, and strength. I always asked for His peace to bring my mind back to the true Darcie—to my true inner self—not to the bipolar Darcie. And each time, He brought back my sanity.

If my medication ever feels off a little bit, usually due to stress, I go in right away for a blood test and fix the problem. I learned through my experience at Harvard's McLean Hospital that I never want to go back there. Speaking for myself, I will not undergo ECT ever again. I have trouble with my memory from day to day. I know some of it is a side-effect from the medications; but no one can convince me that ECT doesn't have a powerful effect upon individuals' memories.

So I now have a very strong will to stay sane and stay alive.

I also had to learn to let go, and to understand that my walk in this life is—and always will be—different. God allowed a lot of heartbreak and suffering to happen, which made me stronger. Some of us will suffer more than others. Suffering, I believe, eventually brings us to that place of true inner peace. When you can learn to lose the most precious gifts in your life, even when you have a sickness, you find out that you have a choice: You will either find your true self and your true needs, or you will self-destruct. *God's goal is always for us to have inner peace! Take the good from this world, and leave the bad.*

In my experience with my inner soul, I truly know that my family does not want me to wallow in sorrow over their deaths, or to let bipolar madness overtake me. They want me to thrive. I know God wants me to continue following Him wherever it takes me. I am never alone if I have God's path to follow. He stays with me each step of the way and shows me which path to take. At times I can feel so lonely; but writing can take away a lot of loneliness for me. I have something to write *about*. It's been an incredible journey, even if filled with a lot of pain. I know bipolar has changed my whole view on life and death. Death should not be a choice we make for ourselves. God will make it for us when He is ready. He always guides our way.

Chapter Twenty-three

Test of Courage

Our Journey in this life is predestined—not by us, but by God. He holds the key to our world and our existence. I have accepted this fact of destiny. I was predestined to have bipolar, to suffer from the cruelty, madness, and sadness of this disease. The predestination of cancer will most likely taunt me the rest of my life, as I'll always be wondering when it may show up somewhere else. With bipolar, I have some control over this part of my destiny, if I commit to my regimen of medications, exercise, doctors, and my spiritual connection. This is something I will always choose to do. Although bipolar will tempt us in certain areas of our minds, we do have some control. Not so with cancer; I do not have any control over the outcome. I maintain the same spiritual connection, and I will continue to take care of my body physically to increase my chances of non-recurrence.

CR

In 2012, this fear of cancer would sneak up on me again. I was having trouble with extreme hoarseness. I went to an ear, nose, and throat doctor. She told me that the right side of my vocal cord was paralyzed, and she wanted to do a CAT scan. A few weeks later, after waiting with much anxiety, I had the scan done. I called and called after that. I did not receive any response from their office, and becoming very frustrated. I found out that the doctor had sent my scan over to my oncologist. When the oncologist received the report, she asked that a biopsy be done on five lymph nodes in my neck and throat. Two weeks later, I was still waiting for the biopsy. They had to perform another scan to see if something had enlarged. I was basically in the dark for a little while. Since the last scan, all five had enlarged on my right side, one pressing on my vocal cords. One had almost doubled in size, so the oncologist wanted them all removed. Finally the ear, nose, and throat surgeon set up the surgery, and I had the lymph nodes removed. One was on my jugular vein and had doubled in size. They could not remove that one. So it had to remain. The oncologist wanted another scan done to make sure they were all okay and taken care of, and it turns out that all was well. My voice came back, and everything was fine. *Thanks to God*!

Chapter Twenty-four

The Reality of this Disease

With all of the craziness in each chapter of my life, with its constant ups and downs, and many losses, it has never been an option to take the easy way out and simply give up. Who would I be, if I did? How would I be there for the most important people in my life?

Bipolar has been very cruel to me. It's taken away family, my friendships, so many people in my life whom I thought would stand by me through thick and thin. The men in my life were obviously not for me; I do know that someday, my true love will wander into my life, and he'll stay through the madness, sadness, and extreme emotions. He'll be strong enough and smart enough to realize that those extreme behaviors and emotions aren't me, but the disease.

Yes, we who suffer from the wrath of this disease know that it can try to take our very lives, our spirit, our soul. The mind seems to take control, and then the craziness moves in circles of racing thoughts, confusion, and irritability. Those of us with bipolar cannot downplay the disease, and should never feel that we have to. It is what it is. It is most hurtful to family and friends, but even more hurtful to ourselves. If we allow it, heartbreak and shame can become our life, as it did mine for a time. We are not to blame. This illness goes far beyond my own understanding. I only know that I have to live with it day to day on its terms.

I am strong when I need to be. I still cry at times, asking why I have this affliction. This frustration is normal. Bipolar disorder is not like any other illness, so all of us stricken with it are special. It may seem funny that I say that; but it's true. If, one by one, we can show the world how to deal with it, then maybe one more person with this disease will be saved.

Suicide is all too prevalent among sufferers of bipolar. As more of us arm ourselves with medication, exercise, spirituality, and a therapist, we can set a good example for those desperate to take their own life. We can start to move mountains. The more we show that we can be strong when we need to be, the more we may be able to help others escape their suicidal thoughts, and decide to get help. I wanted as normal a life as possible, and I have obtained it. If we can all obtain it, then the stigma will start to dissipate as well. *We can stay strong and alive through anything. Let's let our true inner self be our guide, not bipolar.*

Epilogue

When I was first diagnosed, I read one book that really transformed me. Reading it made me realize that I am bipolar (also called manic-depressive). It's called *An Unquiet Mind* by Kay Redfield Jamison. She tells her story of how she has lived with manic-depressive illness for years, while also a professor at John Hopkins University. She is a huge inspiration to me. If I could meet her, I would have an awful lot of questions for her. In the book, she describes her experience with bipolar disorder, and tells about how she also taught psychiatry. This book has been at the top of my list for eight years now. I highly recommend it. Also, I suggest you watch her fascinating talks about bipolar on YouTube.

CR

Looking at the disease from another perspective, I recognize that I have had to learn how to feel. With bipolar, we often want to suppress our feelings, as they may affect our stability or make us experience too much sadness. I came to realize that, for a while, I wasn't feeling, or grieving, as much as I needed. If I hadn't finally let myself feel what I had lost, I would not have seen what I could gain. I learned to love—truly love, like I had never been shown before. And, I found the importance of forgiveness. Forgiveness is vital for our health. I believed I needed to forgive, but I never had to forget. Forgetting devastating things in my life will never be possible for me. Choosing to forgive certain individuals, I have made peace with each person and peace with my inner self. Learning to process my most painful feelings—of fear, sadness, and rejection—has helped me to see the difference between bipolar feelings and emotions. I now understand what true emotions are.

ભ

Writing this book has been the hardest thing I have ever done. I had no idea that journaling was actually preparing me to write this book, and I didn't know what this would do to me, nor how valuable it would be for me. I spent hours crying while typing, as I watched my life of insanity unfold—death by death, page by page.

This narrative is not meant to be all about the deaths, the cancer, the mania, or the hypomania. It is meant to be about one person with bipolar sharing her life with another, and how I have determined what I need to do to survive this disease. We should never go judging people with bipolar as one person being more sick than another. If any of us struggle with this disease, we must try lifting up each one of us who has fallen. Society wants to give us a label, saying we're crazy, and unstable, and that we will all commit suicide. But we will *live* with this disease. That's right—*live with it*—and not ever let it get the best of us. We will *not* die way before our time.

It's a paradox: Nothing is certain in this life, except uncertainty. Who are we, to dare to take our own life, and to make our loved ones suffer immensely? A supposed escape by suicide is unnecessary. *Right now, we have all we need to stay stable*:

- medications
- exercise
- therapist
- psychiatrist

- enough sleep
- spiritual connection

Here are also some coping statements, affirmations that can help us stay in the moment:

- This feeling isn't comfortable or pleasant, but I can accept it.
- I can be anxious and still handle this situation.
- This isn't an emergency. It's okay to think slowly about what I need to do.
- This situation is not the worst thing that can happen.
- I deserve to feel okay right now.
- I am okay right now.
- Let go and relax, there is no need to push.
- Breathe, breathe, and breathe. Connect with your inner self.
- Stay in the present. Talk yourself down from the insanity of this disease.
- This, too, shall pass.

When talking with someone new, I have a tendency to spill out everything. If I do this, I make myself vulnerable, and extremely uncomfortable. Then I notice that the other person I just met has not said one word about themselves. Guard yourself closely, and keep good boundaries. This journey will always be a struggle. I had experienced acceptance in my past from most people, but now I realize that in light of this disease, they don't look at me the same way.

Bipolar is about the will to stay stable and the will to live. Some of us become so angry about having this disease, we may think the answer is drugs, alcohol, or suicide. I promise you, they are not the answer. Instead, *be a light to the world.* Find your unique and healthy way to cope as an individual with this disease. *Live as happily as you possibly can, and others will follow.*

My mother had a will to live; my father had a will to live. Not any of the tools we have could save them. On the other hand, if you have bipolar, *these tools will save you.*

My sincere thoughts and prayers are with you, in every step, in every twist and turn of your journey. It is a good one. It is worth it.

With deep sincerity,
Darcie Cooper

Bipolar Disorder Resources

Numerous hospitals are available. Even if you are suicidal just for one night, don't be afraid to check yourself in. It is not a reflection on you. It's only the disease.

Here are helpful resources you can find easily on the Internet. Find a local group near you:

NAMI (National Association for the Mentally Ill)

Bipolar Disorder Resource Center

Depression and Bipolar Support Alliance

Dialectical Behavioral Therapy—Find a DBT group near you. DBT is wonderful for helping us to stay in the moment.

Here are helpful books you can find easily for sale on the Internet, or in your local library or bookstore:

Mindfulness for Bipolar Disorder. This is a book written by William R. Marchand. Followed consistently, it will reduce stress on a daily basis.

Preventing Bipolar Relapse. This is a good book by Ruth C. White.

The best tools I know of are in this book: *The Bipolar Survival Guide: What You and Your Family Need to Know*, by David J. Miklowitz.

An Unquiet Mind by Kay Redfield Jamison. A definitive memoir by a professor of psychiatry who is also bipolar.

Closing Words of Encouragement

Peace I leave with you; my peace I give you. I do not give to you as the world gives. Do not let your hearts be troubled, and do not be afraid.—John 14:27

Living at the heart of faith is living with uncertainty. Yes, we live with uncertainty. Trust God with each new day so that you become at peace with your uncertainty, open to new possibilities.

Give God a willing heart and a truthful Spirit. He will lead you to peace.

In the dark and dreary nights when the madness is at its most fierce, think of the power you know you have in you to overcome.

Hope is the companion of power, and the mother of success; for whosoever hopes has within him the gift of miracles.

It is faith alone, in Christ alone, which alone moves God when you are alone.—Rex Louis

I live in today, not in tomorrow.

God's will is my guide. I will be ready when He chooses to take me home.

God gives us abundant love through His grace.

Live with a fearless heart. Life is forever changing.

On days of grey and darkness, it's only clouds that block our view. Never give up.

Surrender to the life you have been given, and accept what is.

Our world is not at peace. We have to choose to have peace within ourselves.

No prayers go unanswered, and no one walks alone.

Our journey on this earth was intended to be simple.

CPSIA information can be obtained
at www.ICGtesting.com
Printed in the USA
FSOW01n1400211015
12432FS